Boat Docking

Close Quarters Maneuvering for Small Craft

or

Boat Skidding with Nonchalance

or

Help for the Dysfunctional Docker

-by Charles T. Low

Harvey Island Enterprises
Ontario, Canada

Boat Docking
Copyright © 1997-2006 by Charles T. Low
(Harvey Island Enterprises)

Low, Charles T., 1954-
    Boat Docking : close quarters maneuvering for small craft : or, boat skidding with nonchalance : or, help for the dysfunctional docker

ISBN: 0-9682327-0-1

    1. Boats and boating. I. Title

GV777.5.L68 1997   623.88'231   C97-900623-6

First printing: September 1997
Second printing: December 1998
Third printing: July 2000
Fourth printing: May 2002
Fifth printing: May 2004
Sixth printing: Feb 2006

Harvey Island Enterprises (Publications)
163 Ormond Street, Suite 168
Brockville, Ontario Canada K6V 7E6
fax: 613-342-0232
ctlow4@boatdocking.com
www.boatdocking.com/

-printed by Henderson Printing
Box 353, 1640 California Avenue, Brockville, Ontario, Canada K6V 5V5
phone: 613-345-0411 — 800-263-2655 — fax: 613-345-1949

Boat Docking

— INTRODUCTION —

Boat docking is difficult. Many a boater has decided that the beast has a mind of its own, with little predictability or consistency to its handling. This, of course, is not so.

The problem with boat docking distils to this: boats do not go where they are pointed. Think of a slowly moving boat as always skidding. The vessel is at the interface of two fluid media, water and air. Neither attaches to the boat very firmly, and yet each exerts a strong influence on it, and interacts with the other in complex ways.

Simply accepting this basic tenet, that boats can and do slip and slide in any direction, is half the battle. It all begins to be more understandable if we lose the preconception that it even should go either straight ahead or astern. It should not. It is afloat, not on wheels. It is going to skid.

How a vessel skids is not always very obvious, and that's really why we're here: to learn boat skidding. The techniques for mastering it are often initially counter-intuitive. Coaxing a boat into its dock may well be the most difficult of small craft handling skills, and is usually the one with the largest audience! It can be very embarrassing (or, when done well, gratifying)!

We will be discussing many, many different forces which can prevent your boat from going where you point it, and at first you may wonder how anyone ever gets a boat anywhere. *It will come as a pleasant surprise to see solutions that are both simple and immediately usable.*

This book explains and illustrates the principles of slow speed, close quarters boat handling, and applies equally well to all small craft, regardless of size or type. It will help novices learn how to dock, and will assist experienced boaters to hone their skills, with a better understanding of how they do what they do! The intention is to help you protect your property (and others'), your safety, and, not least by any means, your ego.

There is a short overview section, followed by many practical docking examples and illustrations, and then, for those with a deeper interest, chapters on more advanced and theoretical topics, using non-technical language.

By all means pursue other avenues of boating education. Read the larger reference works, and take a local boating course. I do not think, however, that you will find a more complete and focused discussion of boat docking than that presented here.

Don't feel that you have to read the whole book at once! It can be digested in a single evening, but actually contains a great deal of information for such a small package. You may prefer to tackle it in smaller segments, or to refer back to it piecemeal, comparing it with your own boat-handling experiences.

The Underlying Philosophy

Docking a boat gracefully and comfortably is surely one of the most gratifying yet elusive things a boater can do. Although it is often done well, still it remains a universal nemesis. Despite the very real hazards of the high seas, the more everyday concern of many small craft operators is simply getting their vessels safely berthed. It is very common for docking to be the biggest boat-handling concern a boater has, and to be the most limiting factor in his or her use and enjoyment of the vessel.

What a surprise for the novice boater to find that the vessel does not go where it is pointed! It seems docile enough out on the open water at cruising speeds, and yet develops an independent and capricious spirit in more congested conditions at slower speeds, especially in a wind.

By referring to boat docking as a 'universal nemesis', we recognize that everyone has had some trouble docking his boat, if only on occasion, and everyone, however expert, always still has something to learn. Problems with boat handling are commonplace, and serious problems occur frequently enough that many boaters have witnessed several episodes of boats completely out of control, damaging property and causing bodily injuries.

Among the many excellent boaters who manage their boats intuitively, with grace and panache, some are able, and some not, to explain their methods. Some may be 'naturals', whose main purpose in life is either to annoy us or to inspire us, depending on the kind of day we are having. The more typical seasoned skipper, however, has made many gradual transitions, starting perhaps in early childhood with rowboats, canoes, and small sailboats, only going out in calm, daylight conditions. She or he has progressed through small outboards on open boats, and small daysailers. One day, years later, when we see that he can single-handedly nestle a large yacht in a brisk wind into a tight berth with seeming ease, we may not immediately recognize all of the years of experience behind the maneuver. Much can be learned by observing his work, and by asking for (and taking!) his advice.

Beware, of course, of casual docking instruction from just any boater. There are goodly amounts both of information and of misinformation to be found up and down the docks. Practise healthy skepticism, and choose your advisors carefully.

The Overall Idea

The attraction of the water, and of boating, is indefinable but undeniable. (It's like love.) Whether a sail or power aficionado (and I favour the one that you do), recreational boating provides a healthy dollop of fun and relaxation. We are able to, and indeed have to, forget the cares of the day, and focus on the activity at hand. It can be great training for children, as much on the personal as on the technical level. It brings with it the satisfaction of skills mastered, and one of those sometimes difficult skills is getting the vessel into its berth smoothly.

The discussion which follows pertains more to boats under power than under sail, so is still completely applicable to sailboats docking under power. Sailboats, in this book, are generally assumed to have their sails down: bare poles, except where otherwise indicated. (Docking under sail is another topic. It demands excellent seamanship skills, and can be a most useful, graceful and elegant method of docking.) Airboats and hovercraft are beyond this book's scope. This in no way is intended to undervalue their utilitarian or recreational value.

Different boats handle differently, so some of the discussions in this book will apply to you and to your boat more than to others. You will be able to decipher, from the text and from experimentation on the water, how applicable which characteristics are to you.

The most important chapter of the book, and the easiest to overlook, may be 'Human Factors'. The impediment to, or the motivation for, improvement is often ourselves and our approach to problems, much more than the weather, the boat or the crew. It is also certainly the most difficult aspect of our close quarters maneuvering skill to assess objectively, but our mental and attitudinal status can be as crucial to successful docking as are our physical techniques.

Docking Practice

Don't be too hard on yourself if you are not a world expert boat docker. Most of us have had at least some of what I call 'vocal' dockings: lots of shouting and exclamations, often directed towards a spouse (a dubious tactic!), bumping into docks and other boats, fending off in a panic, or sliding sideways in a wind towards the rocks.

You may never get to the stage where every docking is effortless. (I haven't!) Like many other things in life, there will always be some challenge to docking, and what a disappointment it would be if there weren't. So, don't think that you can stop learning after your first season, or that you would even want to. The only legitimate way to stop learning more about close quarters maneuvering is to get out of boating altogether.

Once through a difficult (or impossible) docking, the boater has two choices: **i)** avoid the offending maneuver in future, or **ii)** overcome it.

Too often we choose 'option one', and remain shorebound on an otherwise beautiful day, simply because it is too windy or we have too few crew. It may not be the open water that daunts us. Frequently, the hesitation stems from the precision required for docking.

Practice Point

*Practise in **small** boats. Punts, dinghies and canoes are fun, and it won't matter so much if you hit anything!*

If you've traded up to a virtual cruise liner and are having trouble handling it, get back into a row boat, perhaps, and try to replicate the docking situation that is confounding you with your larger vessel. Observe again how a boat drifts, slips, skids, and responds to control inputs.

'Option two' requires us to push our docking skills just a little. Recklessness and abandon are not what I am suggesting. For many casual, occasional boaters, prudence is by far the better part of valor. I advocate a very cautious and conservative approach, and one of the things to know is when a certain procedure should not even be attempted. Either because of the operator's limitations, or because of the boat's, some things are just not possible, or are unreasonably risky. So, if you're sure that the conditions are too challenging for you, then don't go out. Your boat needed a good cleaning anyway, the last time I saw it, so this would be a good time to break out the mops and brushes.

However, you won't get any better at docking by staying on land, so when in *doubt* about your abilities, consider erring on the side of enthusiasm. Having given some thought to your close quarters skills since your last outing, and having done some reading and had some discussion on the topic, and having analyzed some of your recent dockings, you may be willing to take the boat out in conditions just a *little* more difficult than you have tackled before.

Learn something from the experience, something about boats in general and about yours in particular. Try a difficult docking again. Make modifications to your technique based on the information you are garnering. (Don't do the same dysfunctional docking a dozen times the same wrong way; then it's not the boat that's the problem!)

Start on calm days, and practise maneuvering on the open water, far from obstructions, giving yourself lots of room to wander. Gradually, go out in increasingly difficult conditions, taking things at your own pace. *Play* with your boat. Enjoy its idiosyncrasies. You love boating anyway, or you wouldn't be this far, so wheel it around just for the sheer joy of it, learning how it responds to various influences, both internal and external.

As you get a better and better feel for your vessel, and a more accurate instinct for how it handles, you will find yourself using less brute force and more finesse. You will make allies out of things which formerly seemed adversaries, such as wind, current and momentum (and crew, sometimes!). You will learn to anticipate the vessel's actions, and actively to *use* its idiosyncrasies, rather than to fight and rail against them, to maneuver it into its dock.

When all is said and done, one learns how to drive a boat by driving a boat. Book learning and water time go hand in hand.

Driving a boat is an art and a science. The science you partly can learn here. The art you learn at the helm. You, like most of us mere mortals, probably will not have it all perfected after the first day. Be prepared to invest the hours, and expect to continue improving your feel for the boat even for many, many years.

If you practise a particular approach a dozen times, your harbour neighbours may wonder about you, but they will certainly notice your docking improving, and you will feel your confidence building.

Chapter 1
— OVERVIEW —

The meaning of the word 'dock' is a matter of some disagreement. Most properly, it means the actual water area in which the boat is secured, nothing more and nothing less. In popular usage it is a platform to which a vessel is 'made fast' (tied up). An ancient definition for a dock is the hollow in the muck where a boat grounds at low tide; we will not use that one, but it seems that to exclude one or the other of the first two would be to deny the natural evolution of the language. The meaning, in this book, will be clear from the context.

Although a 'pier' juts out from land into the water, and a 'wharf' is built along the shore, and a 'quay' is something else again, it matters little, for the present purposes. You dock against any of them using the same techniques, and we may, speaking colloquially, call any of them a dock.

'Mooring' is another word that engenders different definitions. Some boating etymologists feel that it refers *only* to securing a vessel at anchor (commonly a permanent anchor, such as a 'mooring buoy'). This meaning is by no means universally accepted, and this book uses the broader definition of tying a boat up to *anything*.

Boat in Motion

Boats have six motions, and we will refer to some of them many times when describing the many aspects of boat docking. There are three linear motions: surge, sway and heave. There are three rotational motions: pitch, roll (not shown) and yaw. You may (or may not) also be interested to consider a different subdivision: oscillatory and non-oscillatory. Oscillatory motions, heave, pitch and roll, always return towards their neutral position. Surge, sway and yaw do not necessarily oscillate — the boat could continue to go ahead or to the side, or even in perpetual circles, indefinitely.

Pitching, rolling and heaving, important though they are, receive scant mention in this book. We don't want to oscillate; we want to make the boat *go* somewhere! So, we will be talking about surge, sway and yaw, not necessarily using those terms, but certainly alluding to the concepts. Surge involves fore and aft movement, called 'making headway' and 'making sternway'. 'Yawing' refers to turning and 'sway' to moving side to side (sometimes called 'making leeway').

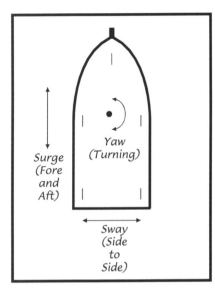

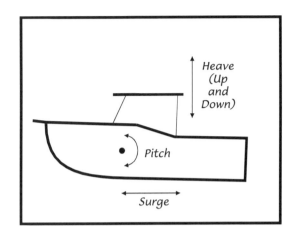

BOAT DIRECTIONS Memory Aid	
Shorter Words	**Longer Words**
left	right
port	starboard
red	green

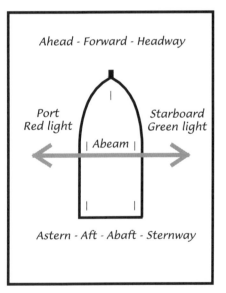

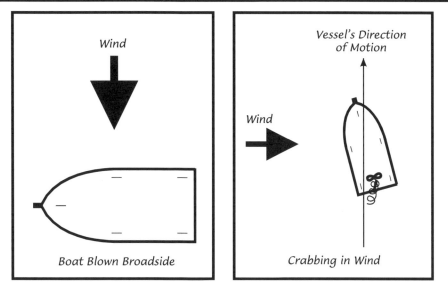

Boat Blown Broadside — Crabbing in Wind

What the Book Covers

Boat Docking deals with the following topics more fully in upcoming chapters.

Go with the flow

There is no particular reason why your boat even *should* head where it is pointed. It doesn't ride on wheels! The hull can and does move and turn in any direction. The trick is to gain an understanding of its behaviour, and then to slide it into its berth under *your* control, not under the boat's!

Forget about where the bow is pointing. This is a very important point, and quite a difficult one. Given that boats 'skid' like crazy, and are not attached to anything at all solid, accustom yourself to sliding your boat around. Pay attention to where the boat actually goes; it may bear little relation to where where the bow is pointing. Accept this simple tenet, and work towards controlling 'boat skidding', and you will be halfway to mastering close quarters maneuvering.

Blowin' in the wind

However unlikely it might look, the wind generally tries to blow a boat sideways ('broadside'). Wind also swings the *bow* of many boats more than the stern, and can do so very strongly. So, you must approach your slip cognizant of the wind and of the effects you might expect from it. It may, in some circumstances, help you into your berth. More often it will be a hindrance, and you will take specific measures to deal with it.

To hold a steady track in a crosswind, aim the bow a bit upwind, and slide through the water on an angle.

It usually is easier to steer in a headwind than in a tailwind, and so you can often dock up more smoothly by turning the boat around and approaching your moorings from a downwind direction.

Current affairs

A current is accounted for similarly to a wind, although the handling is not quite the same. This is because a current does not exert any *rotational* force on the hull. The whole body of water is moving, and, as explained later, this all means that you don't hold any rudder to maintain the 'crab'. Again, however, the important thing is that you aim a little upstream (as opposed to 'upwind'), to hold a straight track in a cross current.

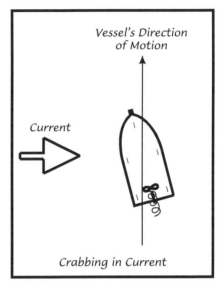

Vessel's Direction of Motion

Current

Crabbing in Current

Momentum control

Momentum is the great unsung hero of the difficult docking. When you shift the engine into neutral gear, or steer the rudder to a neutral position, you are still subject to the force of your own momentum. The boat will continue to slide or yaw for a while. You can use this effect to great advantage, and in fact will often depend upon it, but you *cannot* ignore it. *Use* your boat's momentum. You won't hear boaters talking about this very often, but it *is* a key factor in the *feel* which we develop for handling our boats.

Honourable discharge

The 'discharge current' is the stream of water shot ahead or behind by the propeller, and, in forward gear, it flows by the rudder. This adds great strength to your steering ability. Sometimes, especially at slow speeds, a little shot of throttle can help you to turn sharply without picking up much headway.

Asymmetry

Many propellers, as well as pushing the boat fore and aft, also tend to make the boat turn, for technical reasons beyond comprehension (but explained later in the book!). Most propellers ('screws' or 'wheels') are 'right-hand' ones, meaning that they turn clockwise when viewed from behind in forward gear. These turn the boat to port, meaning that in forward gear, the stern swings to starboard. The effect is often much stronger in reverse gear, in which the stern swings to port. In reverse gear at slow speeds, some boats cannot turn to starboard (or, with a left-hand propeller, to port), no matter what the helmsman does.

Asymmetrical thrust can be a nuisance, although you can often use it to advantage, and even when not, you need to know what limits it places on your boat's maneuverability.

Forward gear to steer

Many boat hulls have difficulty making sternway in a straight line. Add the wind, current, momentum and asymmetrical propeller thrust, and you have a problem. So, align the boat in *forward* gear before making an approach in reverse, making a mental estimate of the effect of all of these forces. Even then, there may be moments when, even while making sternway, you have to steer in forward gear. Slip it into forward for an instant to steer, and then go back into reverse. You may be in forward gear so briefly and/or so gently that you continue to make sternway the whole while (momentum!), or you may actually have to jockey back and forth a bit ('backing and filling'), but you will more likely be able to steer it where you want.

Line dancing

Getting into dock safely and gracefully involves knowing how to use your lines and fenders properly. Not only do we use our lines to tie the boat up, but also, in close quarters, to maneuver it. It's another of those topics that doesn't receive the attention it deserves, partly because when done well it goes almost unnoticed.

Happily, good ties-up are, if anything, easier than clumsy ones, and the basics are simple to learn. It only makes sense that, if we are trying to improve our docking, we give at least a little thought to how to work the lines.

Lines should, in general, be long, not short, and not too loose but certainly not too tight. A properly tied-up boat will always be well 'sprung' and well fendered. The system of lines chosen for your boat will be effective, and yet be quick and easy to secure and to cast off, even in heavy weather or if short-handed.

Home at last

As if maneuvering into position were not sometimes difficult enough, the wind or current will often have you scooting briskly away from the dock, before you can get half of your lines on. This is especially so without crew! You may need to devise one temporary line, which will **i)** be easy and fast, and **ii)** hold your boat motionless enough to complete the more elegant-yet-simple tie-up of which you are so justly proud! Some expert boaters feel that the only option is a line called an 'after bow spring', aided by engine power. Others favour a simpler solution for a small vessel in calm waters: one short line, from amidships to the dock. Best of all, in my humble opinion, is the 'Low-Line', which is described later.

Crew coordination

Thinking of the crew, somewhat coldly, as (just) another of the available tools in your docking arsenal, it follows that we should know how to use it (or 'them'). This comes more naturally to some of us (and I don't mean me) than to others, but it's only an issue at all because we are dealing with humans, not robots. Personally, I prefer humans. We do, as a species, however, have trouble communicating, especially detailed technical information, which often has to be done quickly and clearly during the unfolding of a particular docking maneuver. And that's even before factoring in the emotional overlay that may exist for inter-personal reasons, or because docking in a howling gale can be an enervating experience for skipper and crew alike.

Learning to 'work' the crew is a little like learning how to live life properly - it's a big topic, and we mostly stumble along more or less satisfactorily day by day, and docking by docking. The improvements and insights we gain are sometimes gradual and sometimes sudden, but there will always be room for improvement, and doing it better is better.

Important Concepts

Have a plan. Approach your dock with a plan in mind, but be very prepared to reconsider it at any moment. Perhaps you should come in from another direction, or could use a different steering or throttle technique. You may decide to 'make fast' at another spot, or to go in with the bow instead of the stern, or to use a different technique with your lines. You may need a moment to attract some passers-by to whom to throw lines, or to ask about underwater obstructions or the depth at the dock. Your options will vary with each case.

Be organized. Have your lines and fenders ready in advance. Use fenders generously. If in any doubt, you will not run into trouble by using one more than conventional, nor by having them a little on the large side.

Brief the crew. Tell them what you intend to do, and how you want them to help.

Scout the marina, and see what other boats are under way, or might soon be. Check that the people or objects on your boat will be out of the way of whoever will be working the lines and/or stepping ashore.

Have a back-up plan. I cannot advocate this too strongly. Usually, you design the back-up plan so that if the docking is not going well, you have some way to get out of there, something you have thought of ahead of time, to escape without making an undesired impact. Be prepared to turn away, or to change gears, and clear the area, if need be. Realize that there may be a point of no return, a point after which you must go ahead and dock because you cannot extricate your boat from its position.

Test your transmission and steering, while still out in open water. Shift into reverse, and make sure it works. The same applies before untying and getting under way: just pop into forward and reverse gears for an instant. Apply full helm deflection in both directions. Better to discover a glitch early rather than halfway through an exacting docking or undocking.

Warm up the engine(s). Most engines need not be *right* up to operating temperature in order to function well, but often they need to be run for a few minutes before they can be considered reliable. This pertains mainly to undocking. Among the many variables with which you will be dealing as you maneuver your boat, you surely don't need to include having the engine stall. So keep the motor and all the mechanicals on your vessel in good repair, and remember that 'a warm engine is a happy engine' (thanks, Leonard).

Dock 'incrementally'. Under difficult conditions, you may need several attempts to dock, as you learn how your boat is responding to the conditions presented to it. Drive back and forth past your slip a few times, if possible — all of the turning and maneuvering that this makes you do serves as a last-minute refresher on how your boat (and you) are handling that day in that wind and in that current. Then feel completely free to start and abort a docking a few times (as long as you're getting closer each time!), knowing that your apparent indecisiveness belies a confident, thoughtful, cautious approach towards your approach!

Try to drive right to a stop. This does not mean that you should always power the boat right into its final intended position at dock. Very often, the easier and safer approach is to get it to a location from which the vessel can be walked or hauled in. It does mean that you should try to have the boat motionless, at *whatever* position you choose to cease using engine power as the motive force, if only for an instant, before the wind or the current gets its clutches on it.

It should rarely be necessary to stop the boat by human force, whether directly on the vessel, or by straining on its lines. The engines are considerably stronger than we mere mortals, and 'taking all way off' (stopping) is a task that they can do much more effortlessly and safely than can we.

Restrain unneeded assistance. If you have the situation in hand, it is quite acceptable to ask your shore-side assistants politely if they would not mind just standing by, in case they are needed. They often join in good-naturedly, and interfere with your brilliantly conceived docking plan.

KEEP DRIVING THE BOAT! Manage your steering and throttling *moment by moment*. Nothing is more frustrating than watching someone try to dock by formula, setting the controls, and then leaving them while the vessel wanders off its intended course. No! Make continuous, smooth, small control adjustments, and put yourself right on the money.

Stay at the helm. Resist going to adjust lines and fenders, for example, unless you are very sure that the boat will not drift into danger while you are gone, and that you can return to the controls quickly and safely, should you suddenly need to do so.

Never jump from a boat to a dock. Maneuver at least part of your vessel in close enough for someone to *step* ashore, and the slower the boat is going the better (stopped is best). Slipping occurs commonly, and the crew has been known to fall through a rotten dock board!

Teach your crew how to operate your boat. It is hard to relinquish the exalted status associated with the hallowed helm, or to trust anyone else enough to hand over the reins to your prized steed. It is important, though, and not only because you should try crewing yourself once in a while, seeing how the ordinary people live, but also because you will only fall ill or get injured in bad weather (it is a rule), and your crew will have to get you home and docked. When conditions are less than propitious is not the time for them to be self-teaching close quarters maneuvering!

Chapter 2

— DOCKING EXAMPLES —

Most of these examples assume a single inboard engine vessel. It's a useful model for analyzing boat handling. In some ways, an inboard is harder to maneuver, and in some ways easier, than other propulsive arrangements, whose distinctions, where important, are explained later.

There is no exact formula for any docking situation, despite the somewhat dogmatically presented techniques which follow. Variations in dockages, boats — and skippers — preclude rigid adherence to one policy or another. There are often many solutions to one particular problem, and frequently the solutions are quite dissimilar! So don't be alarmed or surprised when you see successful dockings which bear little resemblance to those presented here. We may both be right. Consider these examples as *suggestions*, as techniques which have served well for many excellent boaters before us. You and your boat will be able to use most of them, and undoubtedly you will eventually adapt many of them to suit your personal style and circumstances.

Often, you will find yourself in *mixed* conditions, such as in a quartering wind, or in opposing wind and current. You will then need to interpolate between various of the proposed maneuvers which follow. If your boat has the less-common left-hand propeller, you will need to reverse port and starboard in many of the discussions which follow.

The examples mainly discuss wind effects. Although the effects of current are not identical, the general principles apply similarly.

Having and using crew and 'longshorepersons' can make life a lot easier, but for purposes of instruction, many of the examples which follow will assume single-handling the boat right into its dock. In real life, however, if the conditions are difficult, the best and safest docking might involve crew, either to fend off the bow, or to throw or carry lines ashore.

Let's assume, for purposes of instruction, that all of the docks we will be discussing are 'tight': there are vessels or other obstructions nearby, so you have to aim for a specific spot, and you have to get it right the first time.

Basic Docking

Front in on the port side

This may well be the easiest docking situation imaginable, so if it is available and suitable, use it! Docking 'port side to' illustrates many of the essential elements of controlling a boat in close quarters, and can be used as the foundation on which everything else is built. If there were only one thing I wanted to impart, this is it.

We're assuming no wind or current at all, for the moment — *that* discussion will appear within a few pages.

The *port* side is specified because propellers behave differently to one side than they do to the other. The more common *right*-hand propeller (see the 'Steering' chapter) tends to turn the boat to port (swinging the stern to starboard in forward gear and even more strongly to port in reverse gear). For left-hand propellers, reverse left and right, and think of this as docking 'starboard side to'.

Firstly, come in at an angle, thirty degrees often being suggested [Diagram 2-1]. In the absence of wind and current, you will be down to bare idle speed ('dead slow') while still some distance out. Get it all lined up, aiming the boat at a spot somewhere in the middle of its intended eventual position. Keep driving the boat, adjusting steering and throttle, because it will not *stay* all lined up, boats being as they are.

Secondly, coast, then, **thirdly**, reverse. Do these while, **fourthly**, swinging the stern in. It really is almost that simple. Still — let's look at it more closely.

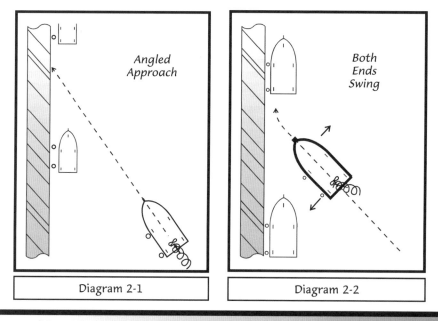

| Diagram 2-1 | Diagram 2-2 |

Angled Approach

Both Ends Swing

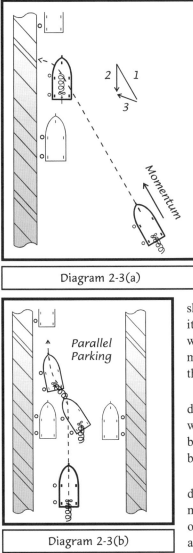

Diagram 2-3(a)

Diagram 2-3(b)

How and at what point do you swing that stern in? Well, with a right-hand propeller, asymmetrical propeller thrust may, in reverse gear, 'walk' the stern to port and be all that you need. If not, remember that steerage may be minimal just at the point where the vessel has lost most of its headway, so you want at least to start swinging the stern in while the vessel is still going ahead [Diagram 2-2]. You may be in forward gear, you may be just coasting in neutral, or you may even have just shifted into reverse, but the important thing, in terms of starting to swing the stern in, is that you are still making headway. Once you lose headway, it may be very difficult, if not impossible, to steer.

It is surprising how closely you have to let the bow come to the pier *if* you are going very slowly. A common error is to start the final turn too far out, forgetting that the boat swings at *both* ends as it steers, and that, at very slow speeds with the rudder hard over, short bursts of power usually yaw the boat as much as propel it. So, as the stern swings *in*, the bow swings *out*, and you will be all nicely lined up — except that you will be one or more arm's lengths from the dock. Go in more closely, and the boat will end up right within stepping distance of land.

There is a visual illusion to how far the bow is from the dock. From the helm, it looks like you are about to collide, when, in fact, you still have a healthy expanse of water between your bow and the dock. (Fly-bridges minimize this, because they look down on rather than over the boat.)

If you have to approach a little faster, the situation is different. Turn a little sooner. Notice [Diagram 2-3(a)] how momentum which has been established *before* the turn (1) is only partly counteracted by reverse *thrust* after the turn (2), and so continues to propel you dockwards (3). The dotted line and arrow in this diagram shows the boat's course of travel, not the direction the bow faces. The hull itself will end up aligned parallel with the dock, 'skidding' into position. Beautiful!

Very often, you won't have the luxury of a long, unobstructed run into your slip [Diagram 2-3(b)]. Dockward momentum will be missing. Depending on your speed (the slowest possible!), turn early and hard enough to counteract forward momentum, and to develop some motion towards the dock. Then proceed as above.

If you actually do contact the pier as you are docking, your fenders will bounce you away from it again. Thank goodness for fenders, but you don't want to bounce away, you want to stay in close. So the ideal maneuver puts you very close in, but not quite touching, and absolutely still in the water.

The timing and vigor of these various maneuvers will vary by vessel, and you learn them only by experience. You won't be able to do it well just by reading it here (although I hope it helps!). Eventually, the whole docking can be done at idle speed, using only one shift of the transmission. This makes it *appear* to be effortless and completely without drama. Almost no one will know how clever you really are. It may or may not be hard to do well, but it certainly can be difficult to make it *look* easy!

With outboard engines, or with twin screws, your options are more open, but more on this later.

Front in on the starboard side

This differs from docking port side to mainly in that asymmetrical propeller thrust will not help you perform the final swing-in of the stern, and may in fact hinder. So, you have to use other means to swing the stern in, and may have to swing it in quite vigorously to compensate for the sideways 'walk' of the reversing propeller.

How to swing it in depends on how your boat handles. The key may be to use reverse gear very gently (which means that you have to come in very slowly, or start using reverse farther out, to allow enough time to stop the boat!). Or, start the stern swinging *before* engaging reverse gear, either while still in forward gear or while coasting prior to reversing. This is similar to that described in the previous section of 'port side to' docking, except that it will have to be done more vigorously.

Having started the boat yawing, depend then, on your boat's angular (rotational) momentum to complete the swing, and to overpower the asymmetrical propeller thrust.

With an outboard or sterndrive, the stern can be pulled in almost equally well to port or to starboard, while the boat decelerates with the engine in reverse.

Docking into the wind

Wind is the most common factor which will make your docking more difficult. In a *head*wind, the suggestions above still stand, except that you will aim a little further along and/or approach at a shallower angle [Diagram 2-4]. Notice that the boat does not follow its nose — you will noticeably crab, or 'skid', during most of this docking maneuver. You *may* need a little more power, not only to make headway but to steer enough to keep the bow from blowing off. In a wind, you may need to stay in gear, and coast less, to maintain steerage control. So, you could be moving a little faster, meaning

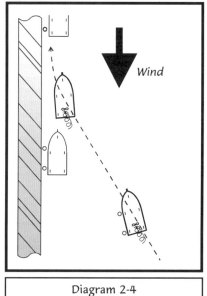

Diagram 2-4

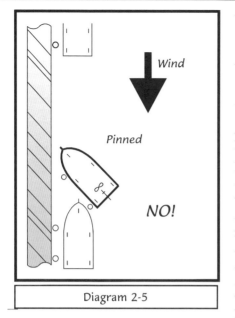

Wind

Pinned

NO!

Diagram 2-5

that you have to think further ahead. Still, you can sometimes steer well in a headwind while going very slowly through the water, which is a nice, controlled way to bring a boat in.

If you come in at too sharp an angle or aim too far aft, you may find yourself pinned in a corner [Diagram 2-5]. There is no elegant way out of this predicament, so it is best avoided. Also, it is very easy to come in too hard, banging heavily into the dock. Despite the air moving *parallel* to the dock, everything else about this docking pushes you towards the dock: the wind blowing on an angle against the hull, and the greater speed which may be necessary for steerage. Also, because the wind is always trying to yaw the hull, the rudder has to be held a little bit over, which i) gives the vessel a littl more *lateral* movement through the water, and ii) means that, at the last moment, you may have to steer even harder to starboard to align the boat with the dock, and this pushes you again more forcefully dockwards.

All of these things are manageable. As long as you know about them, you will be better able to make the appropriate allowances. Aim forward, keep the angle low, straighten out early and straighten out *completely* (and *pay attention!*). Better to err on the side of turning a little too *little* than too much (although in a stiff blow there's not much room for error). If the bow starts to blow away from the dock at the last moment, it can be very difficult to recover without just driving forward out of the slip and having another run at it from the beginning.

Get your lines on quickly, before the wind gets at your boat! Your first line is a bow line. It will keep you roughly in the right place while you arrange your other lines. Alternatively, an amidships breast line or one of the spring line/power combinations, discussed later, may be helpful.

Docking downwind or downstream

Docking in a light tailwind is fairly straightforward, but a strong blow can make maneuvering difficult, and cannot be taken casually. Many boats steer quite well when making *sternway* into the wind, i.e. going backwards with the wind blowing over the transom, but here we're talking about approaching the dock while making *headway*.

A tailwind is easy to underestimate, because you don't feel it in your face at all, and because you are travelling along *with* it, which reduces its *apparent* speed.

The wind will be helping to push you along, so you may be using less engine power, to prevent excessive speed. So, the propeller's discharge current over the rudder will be weaker, and steering less authoritative. You will have to use reverse gear earlier, and stronger and/or longer; this will affect your steerage, quite possibly adversely.

Often the best thing is to take a deep breath and to fight the impulse to get into dock immediately. Put your mooring gear on the other side of the boat, turn the vessel around, and make fast head to wind. You will sit more comfortabl in your berth with the wind and waves meeting the bow anyway.

A following *current* is something else again, because now, to stop the boat, you effectively have to make sternway through the water just to hold still over the *bottom*! Sternway steerage often being squirrelly, this can be a challenge. (Being *surprised* at a dock by a current you didn't know was there is most unpleasant.) You cannot just stop the boat and then relax — often, you have to keep adjusting the throttle and steering continuously just to hold still until someone (and what if you're single-handling?) gets that first line on.

There is no magic to this. Know how your vessel handles in reverse, have your lines ready, and waste no motion when it's time to tie up!

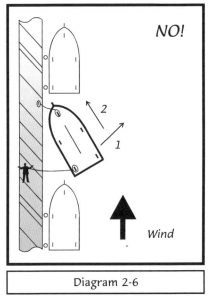

Diagram 2-6

I shudder to recall — well, suffice it to say that I was only an innocent bystander [Diagram 2-6]. This poor fellow put his crew (wife, in this case) on the bow, as usual, to step ashore and attach the first line. He forgot about his tailwind, which blew the stern out away from the dock (1), and then, aided by his deep keel, pushed his bow very forcefully into the dock (2). Two strong men (one of them being me) had to struggle on the end of a long line to pull the stern back in. (There are better recovery techniques, such as walking the bow upwind and letting the stern blow gently downwind, but it wasn't my decision!)

When you do successfully negotiate a dockage stern to wind or current, the simplest line to get on first is a stern line, or an after quarter spring. The boat will stay in the right neighbourhood, and even if the bow floats a few feet out from the pier, you can step ashore from the aft cockpit, holding a long bow line, and pull the bow back in. An after bow power spring (see the 'Lines & Fenders' chapter) is more elegant, and I do recommend it, but it has more potential to go awry, too, especially if you have not had much practice at it. An after double spring (the 'Low-Line') works very well here, too, with or without power.

A favourable crosswind

A favourable crosswind, when docking, blows you towards the dock. Unless the blow is really fierce, just get yourself lined up in position, a leg's length or so out, and let the boat blow in [Diagram 2-7].

Use a little throttle and rudder to maintain alignment, as the wind settles you into your spot. A high-windage boat in a high wind may bump in somewhat heavily. It is difficult to stop the vessel just shy of touching the dock, because it is so easy either to underestimate the

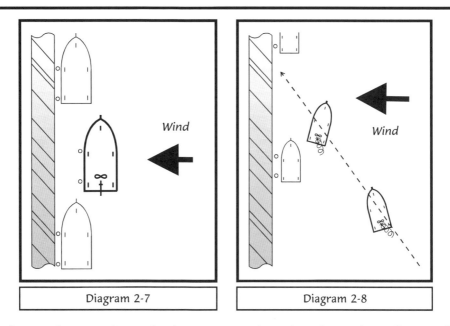

| Diagram 2-7 | Diagram 2-8 |

wind's force, and so come in too closely, or to overestimate it, and come in too far away from the dock.

Also, it may be difficult, as you are slowing to a stop, to keep the higher-windage end (whichever yours is, more often the bow) under control. The solution to this varies widely with the wind and the boat, and often requires the judicious use of momentum. You need enough 'helm-time' that you have a good feel for the way your vessel handles.

Here's a tactic that sometimes works for me: as you get nearer the dock, ready to slow down, actually turn *away* from it [Diagram 2-8]. (Do this far enough out that you don't just ram your stern in against the pier.) At this angle, your last few moments of forward propulsion will partly counteract the wind's lateral force. So, just before you begin to reverse or coast to a stop, your lateral movement towards the dock will be minimal. Now, when the wind begins to swing the bow dockwards, you will be in about the right position.

An unfavourable crosswind

This is surely the most exciting and enlivening situation in which to find yourself. Bringing in a larger vessel when a strong wind is blowing you off the dock, and doing it with style and flair, is what distinguishes you from the casual boater.

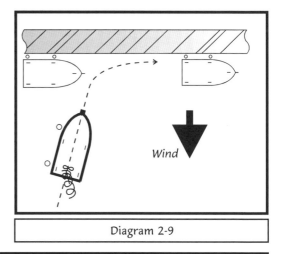

| Diagram 2-9 |

The angle of approach will need to be quite a bit higher [Diagram 2-9] than when conditions are calm. The throttle and rudder need to be used more firmly, although still gently and smoothly.

Bring the bow very close to the pier, aiming further astern than when approaching at a shallower angle. Now turn, but probably a bit less than you would think, for the wind will blow the bow off as the stern swings in. You will make some headway, for which you have left room earlier by aiming further aft.

If you do not do this looking as if you are going to scrape the pier the whole time, you are too far out, and will be blown away from the dock before you can disembark to tie up. If you do scrape — well, I only said to make it look close.

Having maneuvered into approximately the right position, get a line on! The boat will still blow off to some degree, while you are attaching the line, no matter how fast you are. There are many line handling techniques which can serve well in this situation. An after bow power spring works beautifully, and other options are discussed in the chapter on 'Lines & Fenders'.

'Stern to' docking

Docking stern to can be very convenient, especially with swim platforms, transom doors, and cockpits aft. Boarding from the stern is often easier than from the bow. Yet many boaters, while claiming to manage well in reverse, routinely come in bow first. It is more difficult than we will always admit, because so many boats do not steer well in reverse (see the 'Steering' chapter).

If yours, when making sternway, behaves less than ideally, remember the admonition to steer in forward gear. Make a mental estimate of all of the adverse sternway steering factors: wind, current, your momentum, asymmetric propeller thrust, etc. Then, some or all of your initial alignment, prior to actually reversing into your slip, will be done in forward gear [Diagram 2-10]. It is easier, given the standard right-hand propeller, to back to port (because of asymmetric thrust), when turning into your slip. If backing to starboard (as shown), more of the initial turn is done while still going ahead.

When making sternway, you will of course be in reverse gear, or coasting, most of the time, only changing briefly into forward gear when needed for realignment. Even when in forward gear, you will not necessarily be making headway all or any of the time: you may still be going backwards, just using brief bursts of forward propulsion to steer.

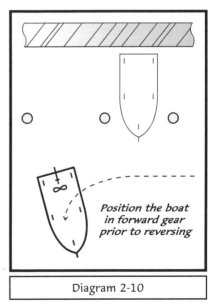

Position the boat in forward gear prior to reversing

Diagram 2-10

Higher Level Dockings

An unfavourable quartering wind

This is a sometimes vexing combination of a tailwind and a crosswind [Diagram 2-11]. The problems therefore are that reverse gear will have to be used longer and/or more vigorously, and yet as you slow down, steerage will be compromised while the wind continues to push you away from the dock.

The handiest docking aid for this is momentum. If ever you needed to *skid* into a berth, this is the time. Come in at an angle, with a *little* more speed than you would otherwise use. The 'linear' momentum you have thus established will help to keep you moving towards the dock, balancing against the wind pushing you away. Start steering into alignment just before you shift into reverse gear, so that there is enough 'angular' momentum to swing the stern in.

You will notice the similarity to the more straightforward 'port side to' docking described earlier. The diagram doesn't do justice to how much more difficulty the wind contributes! The differences in the technique are mainly **i)** the (slightly) increased speed of the approach, and **ii)** the greater rotational force applied before beginning the deceleration phase.

The wind may try to yaw your vessel one way or the other. Know your boat, and put this into the equation when estimating your approach speed and angle, and when deciding when and how much to 'spin' the boat prior to the final deceleration.

Once aligned with the dock, your propeller is now decelerating the boat, but not hindering the sideways component of momentum (as described earlier), and on which you now depend! Pray that your engines do not fail at a critical moment!

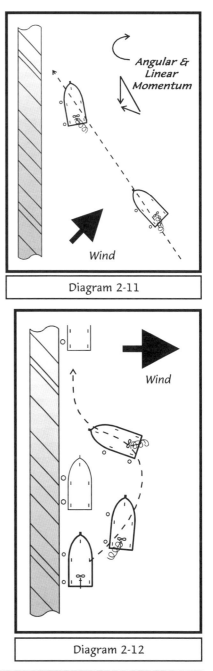

Diagram 2-11

Diagram 2-12

Around an obstacle in an unfavourable wind

The marina manager asks if you wouldn't mind moving your high-windage boat ahead two slips, around a boat already there [Diagram 2-12]. The wind is blowing you off the dock. The amazing thing about this is how high an angle you may have to use to prevent being blown badly off course.

It is easier, although less elegant and more puzzling to passers-by, to do a wide circle in open water, and then to come in using some of the ideas previously presented. But, if you want to exhibit that certain *je ne sais quoi*, then crab past the obstructing vessel, and turn very sharply, sometimes at seventy degrees or more, to avoid overshooting.

Such a high angle is required to counteract the combination of the wind and of your own initial momentum, which is *away* from the dock! Note that, as you leave your first slip, the direction in which the boat will move is quite different from the heading of the bow. Quite clearly, where the boat *goes* is more important than where it points, and this can be a dramatic example of this vital principle.

Sternway in an unfavourable crosswind

This is really living, eh? You try to back into your slip, but the wind blows the bow off. Then, when you try to steer it straight again, of the many ways in which the boat can respond, none helps [Diagram 2-13]. It's difficult enough sliding backwards on an angle through the water trying to track a straight course, but notice then how much you have to turn to begin to edge towards the dock against the wind. As soon as you start to straighten out, the wind starts carrying you off downwind again.

If you have crew, your options open up. Drop somebody off on the end of the finger dock. She can carry a bow line ashore, or be there to catch a line thrown from the boat. Or, if you are backing between piles, you have someone to fend off, and to attach lines, as you manage the controls.

What if you are alone? Well, there are times when you just have to go in frontwards, or walk the boat in by hand from some easier location.

Sometimes, however, you can go in backwards *frontwards*. The idea will be to back in on an angle, still somewhat head to wind, and then sidle up to the pier in forward gear, before the boat is blown completely broadside to the wind.

So, let's say that you are heading upwind through your marina, and want to back into your slip on your port side. As you get near, and how near will be dictated by the conditions and by your experience with your boat, get the stern swinging to port. Use a combination of forward and reverse gears, short bursts

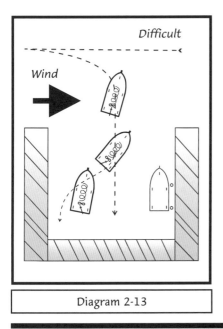

Diagram 2-13

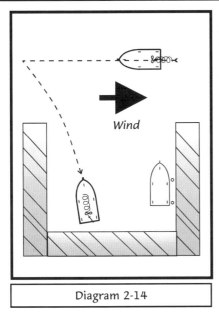

Diagram 2-14

of power, asymmetrical thrust, rudder or outdrive, whatever works for you. The boat should not swing a whole 90 degrees — this time we're going to work *with* the wind, instead of fighting it [Diagram 2-14]. The stronger the wind, the less you want to swing the stern. It does, however, have to go over enough to allow you to move sufficiently backwards.

You can see that in a really good blow you may not be able to back up enough before the wind misaligns you. The trick may be to continue making sternway, but using brief bursts of forward gear, rudder to port, to keep the bow from blowing off.

If all goes well, you will have backed in briskly before the boat has come around quite broadside to the wind. Now, give the propeller a kick ahead, using whatever rudder technique is needed to keep the bow to port, moving it towards the dock [Diagram 2-15].

Then, swing the stern in, as described earlier (see the *'unfavourable crosswind'* section). There you are, you hope, nestling gently against the pier.

It will not be all the way backed in, but well enough placed so that you can get a temporary line on (quickly). Now you can walk it back in the rest of the way, with engine assistance if appropriate, and secure it properly.

Alignment is everything. The pivot has to be done at the right point, and, when first making sternway, you actually may have to aim for the end of the finger dock, expecting to have wind-drifted clear of it by the time you get there. You need plenty of maneuvering room, more room the windier it is. Without enough room, forget it.

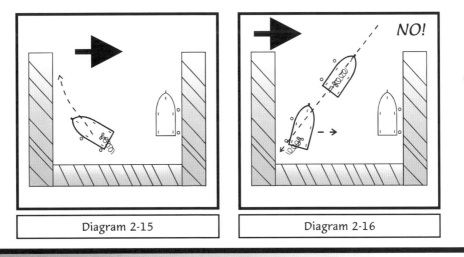

Diagram 2-15

Diagram 2-16

Chapter 2 - Examples

This docking absolutely requires that you have a very clear concept of how your boat handles. Practise easier things first, because doing this well in a stiff blow, even when possible, can require considerable experience.

You might think that you could take an angled run at the dock in reverse [Diagram 2-16], straightening out while stopping in forward gear, letting your boat's momentum continue to carry it sideways against the wind. This is extraordinarily and surprisingly difficult. It looks like a good idea — it just doesn't work very well (without a substantial keel), because the propeller's discharge current (in forward gear, with the rudder to port) augments the wind's effect of pushing you downwind.

Making a controlled sternway docking in a strong cross *current* is virtually impossible.

The blind alley

This is another maneuver which is not always possible. The boat has to negotiate a right-angled turn and yet not move off to either side. There is precious little room for error, and many wise and seasoned skippers will not even attempt it single-handed. However, once again, the principles involved are widely applicable elsewhere. Doing this well uses the concepts of asymmetrical propeller thrust, linear and angular momentum, pivot points, rudder steering and many others.

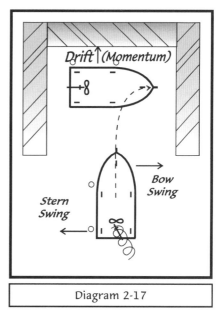

Diagram 2-17

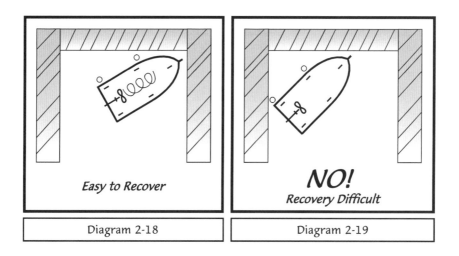

Easy to Recover

Diagram 2-18

NO!
Recovery Difficult

Diagram 2-19

Because of momentum, start your turn further out than seems necessary [Diagram 2-17]. Having turned your vessel, it will still briefly have momentum in its original direction. So, if the wind is calm, you need not power the boat right up to the dock — it will continue to drift abeam, probably quite slowly, and in a few seconds will be within stepping distance of land. (There are many times in docking when the boat will be drifting into the right spot, albeit perhaps very slowly. Resist the primeval urge to *do something* — just wait!)

Because the two ends of the boat will swing in opposite directions, start your turn towards the *middle* of the available space. If you start too far to port (in the previous diagram), you risk impact with your quarter.

It is hard to estimate just when to give the boat that one kick around, and how vigorously and for how long. If in doubt, you are better off starting your turn too soon and too far to *starboard*. If necessary, you can then 'back and fill' [Diagram 2-18], alternating between forward and reverse gears, gradually working your way further sideways towards your dock. This is much preferable and less embarrassing than getting pinned in the corner [Diagram 2-19]. Once there, there is no way out, elegant or otherwise, short of manually fending off or heaving on lines.

In general, if the wind is blowing you off the dock, turn late. The wind will help to turn the bow. With a wind blowing you towards the dock, turn early. In a beam wind, from either side, reassess whether you really want to dock here or not, but if so, start further to the upwind side, making allowance for how far the boat will drift in the wind, and for how much harder it may be to turn the boat at all.

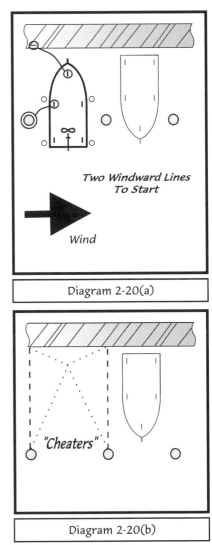

Two Windward Lines To Start

Wind

Diagram 2-20(a)

Diagram 2-20(b)

Pilings

Pilings make efficient (if parsimonious) use of dock space, and are encountered frequently. Lines are thrown over the windward piles as soon as practical [Diagram 2-20(a)].

It is almost certain that the single-hander will have to let a corner of the boat nuzzle against a pile for a moment, however inelegant it may seem, unless conditions are completely calm. So, keep the boat well fendered (although nestling briefly and gently against a wooden piling is not universally avoided). It is comforting if you have a substantial rub rail. You may want to pad your home pilings with fenders, carpet

"Cheaters"

scraps, or other rub protection. Resting momentarily against another *boat* is less desirable, but if completely unavoidable, use lots of big, *clean* fenders between the two hulls.

An experienced boater may be able to lasso one pile while driving, but you need two points of attachment to really control the vessel. You can see how a crew member towards the bow could control the forward end of the boat with lines, while the helmsman *may* be able to manage the other end with power. With one crew, either he or the helmsman attaches the second line, and with two crew you may experience piling nirvana (careful, it's addictive!).

If alone, quickly secure the line which is most easily accessible from the helm station, then hurry slowly (safely) to secure the second line (first shift the engine into neutral gear!), which will be the other line to windward. (Further details on handling the lines are in the 'Lines & Fenders' chapter!)

How to *get* in is another question. Because it is easier to steer when making headway than when making sternway, going in forwards is less of a problem. Many skippers routinely dock bow to between piles, and many others do not hesitate to do so in heavier weather.

Docking amongst pilings stern to, although more difficult, is more convenient, giving better access to the cockpit. It requires a vessel which steers well enough in reverse, and water which is deep enough for your rudder and propeller right against the dock. (The details on steering in are in the 'Steering' chapter!)

Again, do not feel that you have to go all of the way into the slip under power. In a wind storm, it may be better to tie up temporarily only part way in, and then to ease the vessel the rest of the way in by hand.

Note how light 'cheater' lines can be arranged to help guide the boat into its slip [Diagram 2-20(b)]. They can be parallel (dashed lines) or converging (dotted lines), and are sometimes rigged to allow quick adjustment between the two configurations. Just before undocking, the skipper moves the lines in, making them converge. As soon as the boat is back in its berth and made fast, the lines are separated again to their parallel position, so that they won't constantly chafe against the hull, slight though that chafe may be.

Moorings

Securing to moorings, in the stricter sense of tying up to a permanent anchor such as a mooring buoy, has many advantages. The boat floats more freely, tied up only to one line (whose exact length is relatively unimportant), and not against a dock. (The details of how to assemble and anchor the mooring buoy itself are well described in many conventional boating texts, and will not be repeated here.)

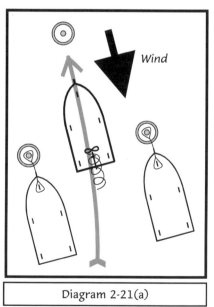

Wind

Diagram 2-21(a)

Getting attached is the sometimes tricky part. You have to aim and come to a stop quite precisely, often with other vessels moored nearby [Diagram 2-21(a)]. Come at the buoy from downwind (and/or down*stream*), of course, and don't be surprised if it takes a little practice to learn how far to coast or how hard to reverse to put your bow just on the spot

If there is a 'pennant', a line left permanently attached to the buoy, then the bow crew picks it up with a boathook, attaches it to the boat, and that's it.

Without a pennant, as at many of the public parks' mooring buoys where I boat, things get more interesting. Somehow hanging on to the buoy's ring with a boathook while trying to reach down and thread a line is obviously possible, because thousands of us do it each year, but in heavy weather it's difficult to do alone.

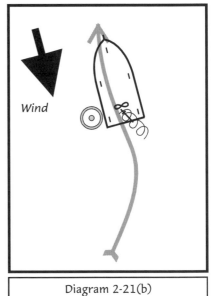

Diagram 2-21(b)

Furthermore, if truly single-handling the boat, with no crew at all, it may not be possible to get from the helm to the bow before the vessel has drifted far from the buoy. In this case, one option is to drive the boat's *quarter* to the buoy [Diagram 2-21(b)] and snag the ring from the cockpit. Then, walk the line to the bow. In very strong winds, you could always tie the line off at the stern, take the 'bitter' (free) end forwards and tie it off there, and then release the attachment at the stern. Lastly, shorten the bow line as appropriate for the circumstances.

Undocking

Undocking is easier than docking. It is almost this simple: if you get good at docking, the close quarters maneuvering skills you have mastered will allow you to undock. Use your knowledge of wind and current, of lines and of engine power, often simply reversing the steps that you use to dock.

There are a few common errors, and the only skippers who have not made some of them are the ones who boat very little. **Warm the engines**. 'Warm engine, happy engine.' **Untie the boat**. Pretty well everyone has tried to leave a berth with a line still attached (or a shore power cord, or a water hose, etc.). Make it a habit to check that you are completely

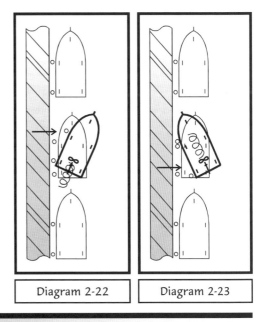

Diagram 2-22   Diagram 2-23

unsecured just before putting the engine in gear. Look right over the gunwales and check for yourself. **Check for traffic** before leaving your slip. For some reason this is often forgotten, on the water. It is impolite and dangerous (and also generally illegal) to cut off a boat already under way.

The dissertation on 'lines', elsewhere in the book, also has some useful concepts which relate to leaving a slip.

If someone is able to push off at the bow [Diagram 2-22], you can go ahead immediately. This affords you the best steerage possible, although you have to be careful to leave enough room to swing the stern as you steer the boat away from its slip. The 'pusher' can be on the boat, on land, or can board the boat while pushing off.

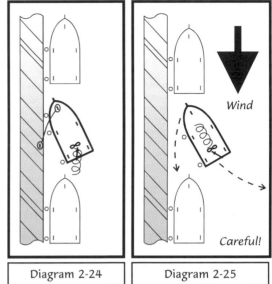

Diagram 2-24

Diagram 2-25

Conversely, back out, first having swung the stern away from the dock [Diagram 2-23]. This swing can be done manually or under power. When done by hand, it allows the single-handed skipper quicker access to the helm than if she had to run all the way from the bow. Pushing off at the stern like this makes good use of the bow's curvature, in that the boat can *pivot* without the bow colliding with the dock.

Now, just reverse in a straight line (if your boat will do that) until enough room has opened up to allow you to maneuver away in forward gear.

You may be able to swing the stern (or bow) away from the dock under power, using techniques described elsewhere in the book, such as asymmetrical thrust, water cushions, or the direct pull of an outboard engine. You can go ahead on an after bow spring (using extra fenders!), with the rudder aligned with the dock or turned towards it [Diagram 2-24], and the stern will swing out, although you will probably need crew to handle the line.

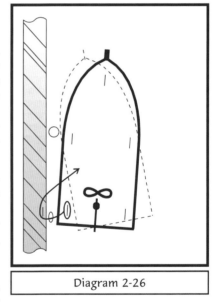

Diagram 2-26

Be careful about backing out of a slip in a headwind — the bow may swing quite quickly, making maneuvering very difficult [Diagram 2-25], and possibly colliding with whatever is astern.

Pulling *in* on a bow or stern line compresses the nearby fender and pulls one end of the boat in closer to the dock [Diagram 2-26] (solid hull outline). Release the pull, and the fender, now expanding, bounces the end of the boat out and away from the dock (dashed hull outline). This little trick can be useful if single-handling, because it can be done from onboard the vessel, and doesn't present the risk of falling between the boat and the dock as you push off. Use a line which is attached to the boat, is looped around the dock's cleat or pile, and has the bitter end back aboard (as shown by the arrowhead). Pull in on the bitter end to squish the fender, then let it go and *quickly* pull the line in from the attached end (the 'standing part'). Don't let it get caught in your propeller! Move promptly to the helm, but wait until the boat has turned enough to exit safely, and then drive away.

A wind blowing you away from the dock makes things easy. Simply drift away from the land, using a little power and rudder for alignment as necessary. If a strong wind is pinning you *against* the dock, however, your usual undocking maneuvers have to be exaggerated, and sometimes greatly so. If not, you may end up back where you started, or colliding with objects ahead or astern. The technique shown [Diagram 2-27] may look unlikely, but in practice often works very well. Some experts advise against it, and it is less applicable to larger boats. Be careful not to ground your propeller or rudder, as the water may be shallowest right against the dock, and not to crunch them into the dock itself. Forward gear is used gently but *authoritatively* — no hesitation allowed! Get the bow out far enough before applying power, so you aren't blown back into the boat ahead!

The use of power spring lines can also be invaluable here, as described above and also in greater detail elsewhere. Still, there are occasions when even experienced boaters have simply been unable to maneuver out of a berth until the wind settled.

Single-handing a twin-engine boat, the bow can be levered off the dock by using forward gear on the dock side, and reverse gear on the other [Diagram 2-28]. Make very sure that the quarter is well fendered, and be prepared to adjust the throttles to keep from sliding ahead. When the desired angle of departure is reached, go ahead on both engines. This works for some twins against even a fairly stiff wind.

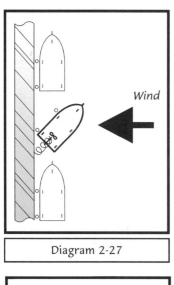

Wind

Diagram 2-27

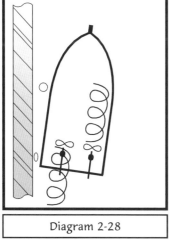

Diagram 2-28

Chapter 2 - Examples

Chapter 3

— HULL EFFECTS —

Hulls

Small craft handling at low speeds can be problematic because of the literally fluid connection between the boat's hull and the water. The boat will slip and slide any old way, not necessarily following the bow. It can and does go forwards, sideways, backwards, [Diagram 3-1], and can yaw, pitch and roll, influenced not only by the propeller, sails, and/or rudder, but by many other factors, including the wind, waves, current, and its own momentum.

Our boats float on top of the water and at the bottom of the atmosphere, and the effects of this air/water interface cannot be over-emphasized. The wind pushes and turns the boat, and a current may drag it off in some other direction. This is even before we begin to consider the mechanics of the hull in motion.

It surely takes considerable skill to fly an airplane, or to maneuver a submarine, but a surface vessel has to contend with both air and water effects at the same time. As some aircraft pilots will attest, maneuvering a boat at slow speed involves its own set of complexities. An airplane is landed while still moving, which admittedly brings with it its own set of challenges. Yet one of the reasons docking a boat is difficult is that the maneuver is done with the boat barely in motion, and thus not very steerable. A boat (or an airplane) is steered by its movement and/or propulsion through the water, and while docking, you may have very little of either!

Modern boat hul ls should generally track well, meaning that, in forward gear at their designed optimal speed, they will steer well, going straight ahead with only small adjustments at the helm, and with minimal 'wandering'. However, their *optimal* speeds and their *docking* speeds may differ by an order of magnitude.

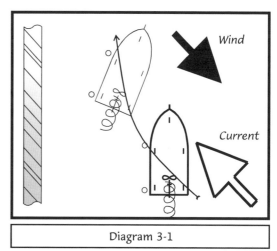

Diagram 3-1

Planing-hull power boats have particular problems in this regard. When 'up on plane', they are skimming over the water's surface, having jumped over their own bow wave. They are built to handle well under these conditions. Docking speeds are much slower. They then will be definitely 'displacing', not planing, and may be much less steerable.

If so, you will have to do a lot more steering, just to maintain your course. It is easy to get carried away, though, over-correcting, weaving and wiggling through the marina. As you get to know your boat better and better, try to steer gently and smoothly, by anticipation and by gentle persuasion, rather than by coercion.

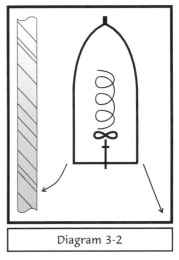

Diagram 3-2

Many hulls do not track at all well while making sternway. Try backing your boat around a small course of some kind, in calm conditions, at different speeds. Depending on its design and on your ability, it may do well, but some hulls just have no particular desire to obey the helm when going astern. This is aggravated by a flat transom, especially if there is no substantial keel, and more so at higher speeds.

The hull may want to treat one of the junctions between the side and the transom as a 'bow', and you can see why it might, if you look at it and think about it for a moment [Diagram 3-2]. This 'non-bow' is not well designed for tracking, so even if you decide to accept the diagonal direction in which it wants to lead you (as illustrated by the straight arrow), it may insist on continuing to turn (shown by the curved arrow). The use of more power and/or speed may only aggravate the situation: the boat may yaw even more violently, completely beyond the control of the rudder.

Beyond this, there are many other factors, which will be discussed later, which may make steering difficult in reverse. So, if your boat, when making sternway, responds promptly and precisely to steering input, just count yourself lucky (and take the credit).

Keels help your boat track straighter ahead (or astern), and lessen any sideways drift [Diagram 3-3]. For close quarters maneuvering, they are almost always good, although a long keel makes the boat less willing to turn tightly. Planing hull boats rarely have keels, and displacement hull boats, especially sailboats, almost always do. There are many design variations, such as deep fin keels in the centre of the hull, to improve maneuverability. The important thing about keels, when docking (other than having to consider their draft), is to recognize their effect on a particular boat's handling.

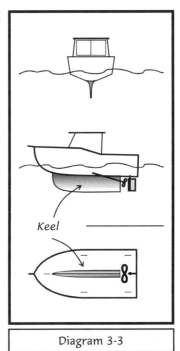

Keel

Diagram 3-3

Wind

For many boaters, the wind is the greatest challenge faced when bringing a boat into its berth. All of the parts of the boat above the water line feel its force, and it is a force to be reckoned with. Even a little breeze of five or ten knots can easily upset your docking plan, and you may encounter much stronger winds than this, depending on your boat, on your skill and experience, and on serendipity.

The example dockings presented elsewhere deal with the mechanics of docking in various winds. This section reviews some of the underlying concepts of wind effects on boats.

Take your boat out into open water, and see how your hull and superstructure drift in the wind. Most boats will end up, after a brief time, more or less broadside to the wind (and waves!), as illustrated in the 'Overview' chapter. They can 'weathervane' to some extent, if one end is lighter and higher than the other, but the water resistance buffers this considerably. It is surprising how quickly considerable sideways speed can be picked up. You may notice some headway or sternway, depending on the interactions of the wind and water with your hull.

Aim gently up into the wind, and again drift. How long does it take for the bow to 'blow off'? Try the opposite going downwind.

Try backing up downwind. This means that the boat will be bow to wind, the engine in reverse gear. Many boats, especially those with minimal keels, simply cannot do this, even twin screws, with their fabled maneuverability. In a strong enough wind, the bow may blow off. Even full rudder may not be able to bring the bow right back into the wind [Diagram 3-4], and the direction of motion may not be completely predictable. (Steering is much more decisive in forward gear.) A low profile displacement-hull sailboat with a deep or long keel will have less wind exposure, as compared with the water forces acting on its hull. It may, therefore, blow off fairly slowly.

At the other extreme is a relatively light, planing power boat. Length being equal, it probably weighs much less than the sailboat, so there is less under the water and more exposed to the wind. The engine(s) and fuel tanks are often heavy, and right at the stern, while the topsides are often highest at the bow where there is little weight and minimal draft [Diagram 3-5]. Both factors contribute to these boats' notorious reputation: their bows blow off rather viciously. If you put up a big camper canvas over the cockpit, the overall 'windage' will increase, although it may yaw (turn) the boat more slowly, or at least differently.

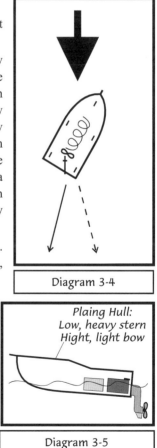

Diagram 3-4

*Plaing Hull:
Low, heavy stern
Hight, light bow*

Diagram 3-5

In between are other hull types, such as small planing sailboats, or larger displacement-hull motor yachts, whose wind effects will be intermediate.

Although commonly thought that a larger boat will be less subject to wind effects than a smaller one, sometimes the converse is true. Do not trade up to a larger vessel, assuming that it will be easier to dock. It may be, but although a bigger boat has more in the water, it often has even relatively more exposed to the wind, such as masts, rigging, cabins, camper tops and fly bridges. All of this is higher above the water's surface, and the wind is stronger up there. Also, more of the boat extends above the actual pier itself, so that there is less of a windbreak.

Furthermore, the pier is often easily accessible from a small boat's cockpit; you just reach out, grab on, and hold yourself there. Larger boats' cockpits are higher, and — well — larger, so the pier is further away, and you may not be able to reach it. The windage may be such that you cannot even hold onto the dock. It is amazing to feel the force of a twenty knot wind broadside on even a mid-size recreational craft.

Watercraft do not propel themselves sideways. (Those of you with bowthrusters or twin screws, please hold your peace, just for a moment. By all means, take full advantage of them, but also learn and practise the basic principles of good boat docking without them.)

Boats *can* be 'walked' sideways (described more fully elsewhere in this book), meaning that by going alternately ahead and astern, steering in small increments as needed, you can pull the vessel to one side without much fore and aft movement [Diagram 3-6], although it's not easy — it's not a natural motion for many boats. It is a bit like getting a car into a tight

Wind Blankets

Wind is often drastically modified, and usually greatly reduced, by structures and objects near to the docking area. This is often all to the good, although it requires an abrupt change in mental conceptualization for just those last few boat lengths into the dock.

The area that is 'blanketed' from the wind in the lee of an island is often said to be seven times the height of the trees. The wind in a dockage area may be subdued not only by trees, but by buildings, by other boats, and by the height above the water of the dock itself.

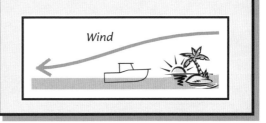

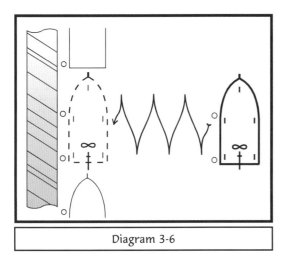

Diagram 3-6

parallel parking spot, only worse. At best, the boat's sideways movement is slow, and the wind can be fast, so walking may not work just when you need it most.

Therefore, you have to crab. 'Crabbing' is not only what your spouse does after you have criticized her or his crewing (essential though this is to the art of boat docking). Crabbing also means pointing your bow in a different direction than the boat is going, to account for wind (or current) [Diagram 3-7]. Your boating technique always has to account for side slippage from the wind. A sailboat, when 'reaching' under sail, crabs all the time; it is called 'making leeway'. A power boat with a small or absent keel is *particularly* susceptible to leeway, especially at low speeds.

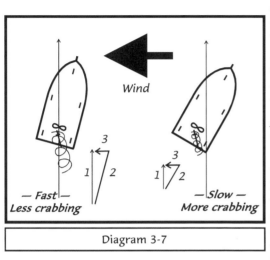

Wind

— *Fast* —
Less crabbing

— *Slow* —
More crabbing

Diagram 3-7

Therefore, if you want to make good a true course broadside to the wind (1), you have to aim the bow up into it. The slower the speed (2), the higher the angle, to counteract the effect of the wind (3). (Remember vector diagrams? — you *knew* there was a reason you went to high school!) The boat hull will actually move *diagonally* through the water to go *straight* over the bottom.

Note that not only do you slide the hull through the water on an angle, to counteract a beam wind, but you have to leave the rudder turned, to prevent the wind from turning the boat, blowing it broadside. You have to 'hold some helm'.

If the wind is gusting, and you are in close quarters, leave yourself some maneuvering room on your leeward (downwind) side. Stay upwind as much as possible, in other words. This leaves your options more open, and affords you room and time to react, should the wind suddenly increase.

The answer, my friend — use the wind as your ally. Often, even if the wind is not helping to *blow* you into your berth, it can help you to *maneuver* into your berth, once you figure out just how the wind affects your vessel.

In general, do as much of your maneuvering as possible *into* the wind [Diagram 3-8]. This will slow your water speed, minimize your windrelated leeway, and allow you to steer better by being in forward (rather than reverse) gear.

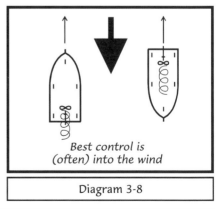

*Best control is
(often) into the wind*

Diagram 3-8

Chapter 3 - Hull Effects

Furthermore, maneuver into the wind even when making sternway. In this case, you just allow the bow to weathervane downwind. Your steerage will be much better than in a crosswind or a 'bow' wind.

Very commonly, a boater finds himself fighting the wind every time he tries to dock. He just needs to come at it from the other direction (circumstances permitting), and let the forces of nature work for him, not against him.

Current

Find dockage where there is a negligible current, for heaven's sake! If this is not possible, bear in mind that there are many places where the current is variable, changing with the tides, the seasons or with adjustments at the spillway. If the current is inconstant, you cannot memorize a formula to manage it. Rather, you have to analyze the situation afresh at each docking, and understand how your boat will handle in the current current!

The forces of the current and of the wind may be additive or subtractive. Furthermore, both can change drastically as one nears shore, necessitating a complete change of steering technique during the approach to a dock or mooring. You often just have to figure this out as you go along, especially in an unfamiliar location. Pay close attention, and be prepared to change your tactics, as Nature changes hers.

Current and wind effects are similar, but differ in several respects. Most obviously, a current acts on the hull below the waterline, versus the wind above. Secondly, water is so much denser than air that its effects are more immediate. The air does little to buffer them, whereas wind effects are strongly buffered by the water.

Because the boat is much more firmly 'attached' to the water than to the air, it tends to flow along with it, not going broadside, the way it often does with wind. For a boat adrift, there may be no particular direction it prefers to face; it will just flow with the current, pointing anywhere. In other words, a current doesn't try to *yaw* the boat.

A boat drifting in a current can be viewed as being stationary in the water, with the land movingby it. If this relativistic concept does not help you, do not linger overit.

Things change as soon as the craft is in motion. The concepts of crabbing, as discussed under 'Wind', apply very similarly to current. In both cases, you go diagonally,

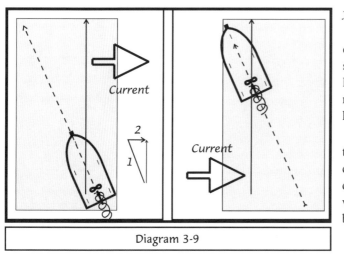

Diagram 3-9

so as to make good a straight course over the bottom. Crabbing in a wind, however, the hull actually moves diagonally through the water, whereas in a current you go straight through the water [Diagram 3-9], as shown by the dashed line, while the mass of water itself moves, as shown by the large open arrows and the shaded rectangles (which move from left to right across the frame). The vessel moves over the bottom as shown by the solid arrows. Notice the pesky vector diagram again — if you're not interested, you can safely ignore it. The boat's propulsion (1) and the current (2) produce the direction of travel as illustrated.

Because there is no force yawing the boat, crabbing in a cross current — vs. a crosswind — needs no particular rudder pressure. You do not 'hold some helm', and so the 'feel' is different.

Another distinction is what happens when you change speeds, as you likely will want to do as the wharf gets nearer! With a wind, as you slow to dock, your momentum may assist you in to dock nicely before the wind gets hold of your hull. The current, so much more tenacious on the boat, will have a more immediate and pronounced effect as you slow down.

Often, the only practical way to control a boat in a significant current, at slow speed, is to head into it. Generally, going ahead slowly into the current, you will make some forward motion with respect to stationary objects such as the land or wharf, and be able to steer yourself into the desired position.

If you get the current coming at you from the side, even only moderately, off you go, with the flow. You have to crab right into the dock, then have the crew get lines attached immediately. Doing this alone in a larger vessel is not impossible, just improbable.

Docking facing downstream is also definitely undesirable, since you will need forward motion through the water to steer. The water itself is moving, so your speed going by fixed objects could be considerable. To come to a stop, you not only have to use reverse gear authoritatively, but actually make sternway through the water. This may entail serious steerage problems.

Estimating the current in advance is a very decided advantage in planning your approach. Observe the direction and strength of the water flowing by piers, buoys or piles.

Momentum

A boat in motion has momentum, proportional to its speed. It tends to keep going in the direction it is going! (If you prefer to think about 'kinetic energy', which is proportional to the square of the speed, please feel completely free to do so!)

Momentum can be an asset or a liability, but ignore it at your peril.

There will be times when momentum is not even perceptible: the wind or current or asymmetrical propeller thrust take the boat off in some new direction. Yet this is where momentum often actually comes in the handiest. Anticipate the unfavourable forces working against you, and set up some momentum in advance to oppose them and take you on to victory!

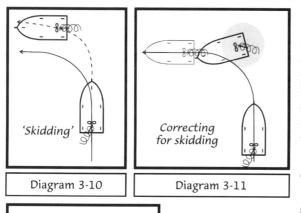

'Skidding'	Correcting for skidding
Diagram 3-10	Diagram 3-11

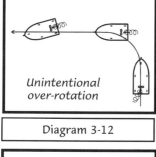

Unintentional over-rotation

Diagram 3-12

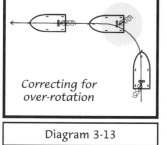

Correcting for over-rotation

Diagram 3-13

Don't underestimate momentum! It is infrequently discussed in the close quarters maneuvering literature, but it is possibly the most under-rated docking tool we have available. Those skippers who seem to just 'feel' their boats into their slips have an intuitive understanding of momentum.

Two types of momentum will be discussed: first, *linear* momentum.

Turn your wheel hard over, at slow speed, and turn your boat 90 degrees. What direction will you now be going? Well, your propeller will be pushing you in the direction the bow is heading, but you still have momentum in the direction you were going initially [Diagram 3-10]. The boat skids (dashed line)! You will go diagonally at first, gradually assuming the direction you intend, as your momentum dissipates. So, to actually make good a sharp turn [Diagram 3-11], you have to start early, knowing that you will slide through it a bit sideways, and possibly point the bow further around the turn than you might think (note the rudder in the shaded circle): 110 degrees to effect a 90 degree turn, for example, and sometimes much more. As the sliding stops, ease back to the 90 degree heading.

Now, *angular* momentum: a boat turning tends to continue to turn.

This means that, having turned the bow to the desired new angle, you cannot suddenly straighten the rudder and expect to hold your heading. The boat will continue to turn for a while [Diagram 3-12]. It is often enough simply to start bringing the wheel back to centre slowly and smoothly, a bit earlier in the turn. Sometimes, though, you have to turn the wheel (and rudder) beyond centre (shaded circle [Diagram 3-13]) and actively stop the boat from yawing further.

The angular momentum may help to overcome linear momentum: by tending to make your boat turn too far, it may help arrest some of the undesired skidding. This will work best if you know that it is happening, so that you are still driving the boat, not it driving you!

A common technique is to apply linear momentum in *one* direction, and then to allow it to continue while applying power in *another* direction. The description of docking in a quartering wind, in the 'Docking Examples' chapter, illustrates this well. You come into

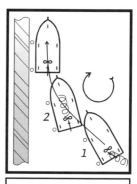

Diagram 3-14

the dock at an angle, but apply reverse gear after having turned the boat parallel to the dock. The perpendicular component of momentum remains unopposed, and carries you on in against the wind.

Or, you can establish *angular* momentum, and then apply linear power [Diagram 3-14]. For example, just the last few moments as you approach a dock, you put the rudder over (1) and set the stern swinging in to the pier. Now, centre the rudder and apply reverse gear (2): your rotation will continue, from momentum, even though your rudder itself is losing effect, as can be expected at low speeds in reverse gear. Skid right on in. This illustration is slightly 'exploded': this maneuver could be expected to occupy less space in the real world, but is spread out here for clarity.

Not Too Shallow

It is a good idea not to get into too shallow water anyway! Although very basic, it is a concept overlooked or taken too callously time and again, until a boat hits a rock and possibly sustains damage. (Some boats on some bottoms and under some circumstances can safely ground.) Water near shore is, of course, often shallow (or tidal, or seasonal), and just because there is a wharf or a pier there, even with other boats against it, does not mean that *you* will clear bottom.

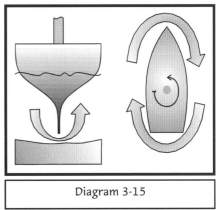

Diagram 3-15

Water depth has an effect on hull behaviour. When there is very little distance beneath the hull, or especially the keel, and the bottom, steering can be noticeably more sluggish. Presumably, this is because as the hull turns, more of the volume of water being displaced now has to be pushed all the way around the ends of the boat [Diagram 3-15], the more direct route underneath now being restricted.

Keeping on Course

One would think it simple to know whether a boat is tracking straight ahead or not. Experience shows otherwise. There are various reasons, including wind, current, momentum and visual perception, for the boat not travelling in the direction the bow is pointing (or seems to be pointing), and deducing the actual 'track made good' is not as straightforward (if you'll pardon the pun), as one might think.

How much crabbing is the right amount (speaking about boating, now!)? Think about where the boat is *going*, rather than about where the bow is *pointing*, and steer by that. You can, of course, observe whether things beside you are getting closer or further away, to tell if

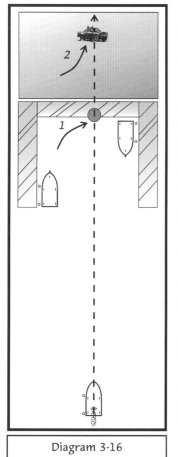

Diagram 3-16

you are drifting off course. But even short distances across the water can be very deceiving, and the sense of perspective quite misleading.

There are more versatile techniques for staying on course. They sound complicated, but quickly become second nature, with a little practice. One method is to line two things up, creating a 'range' [Diagram 3-16]. Sight past what you are aiming at, such as a pile (1) at the far end of the marina, and line up something behind it (2) in the distance. If you keep those two things lined up, then whatever it is that you are doing to steer the boat, and wherever your vessel seems to be pointing, you will be going in a straight line and staying on course. You are making the correct allowance for the wind, for the current, for leeway and for many other confounding variables.

At slow speeds, or if the range marks are too closely spaced, it can take a few seconds or longer to decide whether you are tracking true or not, so don't rush your assessment.

A less precise method is harder to explain. It is a modification of the airplane pilot's 'bug on the windshield' technique [Diagram 3-17], whereby one of the two things with which you line up is on your boat (1). The mark towards which you are aiming should not seem to 'move' sideways along your bow rail. If it moves to port, you are off course to starboard.

This latter technique is less precise because it does not place you on any particular line — the range is simply from wherever you are at the moment to the destination of your choice. It fails if your boat yaws, or if the wind or the current changes — use external range markers, if at all possible.

You may find the use of a range helpful even when tracking straight ahead in completely calm, zero-current conditions, because the helm position is not always over the boat's midline. This creates a very powerful and common visual illusion, in which, in the absence of lane markers, the eye is led erroneously to the point of the bow. This results in a terribly off-course, curving track through the water [Diagram 3-18]. If the helm is to starboard (shown by a steering wheel in this illustration), aiming over the *middle* of the bow causes you to turn to starboard. This is a ubiquitous, under-recognized close quarters navigation error — the illustration is exaggerated for emphasis, but not much!

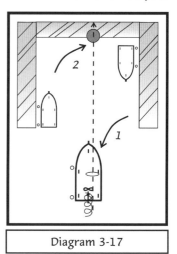

Diagram 3-17

It will probably take some experimentation to decide where, in fact, to aim over the boat's bow to make good a course straight ahead. When you are not centred in your boat, the point dead ahead of you may be surprisingly lateral on the bow. Move your head over a few inches, and your whole forward sight-line moves over too. Use a range, sometime, when there is no current or wind, to track straight, and see how it looks from the helm. You may want to place a piece of marker tape on the rail, in line with the centre of the steering wheel. At cruising speeds you can also use your wake to double check that you are indeed tracking straight ahead.

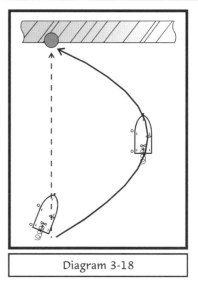

Diagram 3-18

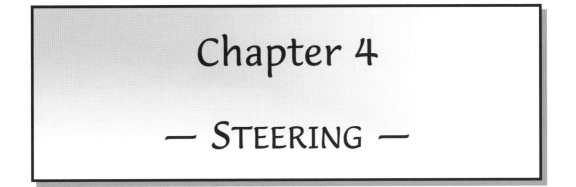

Chapter 4

— STEERING —

Let's start with an examination of steering a sailboat under sail. From there, we can make a logical progression to inboard-engine boats, outboards (including sterndrives [inboard/outboards]), and twin engine installations. We will see how these configurations respond in various situations.

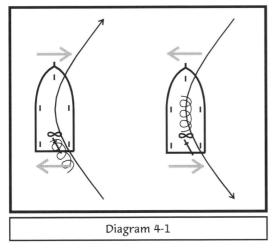

Diagram 4-1

Turning and Swinging

Bear in mind that both ends of a boat swing, when you make a turn. In most situations, one thinks of *turning the boat*, to make it go in a different direction. Sometimes, however, especially when docking, the direction is unimportant — we just want to *swing one end* of the boat a little to one side or the other.

The relationship between the turns and the swings changes depending on whether you are making headway or sternway. The key is simple. Going ahead, if you turn one way, the bow swings in the same direction, and the stern swings to the opposite side [Diagram 4-1]. Going astern, the stern swings with the turn, and the bow swings the other way.

Swing is most noticeable at low speeds, such as those used for docking! So keep in mind, when thinking about boat steering, which way the boat is going, and whether we are talking about the whole boat turning or about one end swinging.

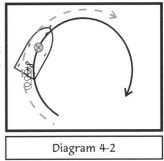

Diagram 4-2

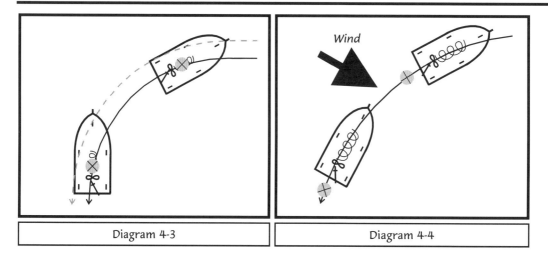

| Diagram 4-3 | Diagram 4-4 |

If this seems completely clear to you on a first reading, perhaps you need to go back and have another look at it!

Swinging is more easily understood if one has an inkling of where the 'pivot point' is ([Diagram 4-2], shaded circle), and you learn where only by observing the boat repeatedly, as it turns. In general, when making headway the pivot point is closer to the bow than to the stern, so it is the stern that swings most (dashed line).

Making sternway, however, the pivot point's location is less predictable, and can move ahead or very far astern, depending on the boat and on conditions at the time. (Technical note: it at least behaves as if it moves.) If the pivot point moves aft, the bow will swing widely as you turn [Diagram 4-3]. The further aft it moves, also, the more sluggishly the boat turns [Diagram 4-4]. This often happens in a beam wind, in which the 'virtual' pivot point can move far aft of the hull, hanging out over the water, as it were — you may try to turn, only to mainly move sideways. The (apparent) location of the pivot point is influenced by many factors, including the hull design, propeller and rudder locations, speed, direction of motion, and rate of turn.

Speaking of swinging, make very sure that you always allow enough room for the 'other' end of your boat to swing! It is all too easy to get yourself cornered, and not be able to get out, as illustrated in other sections of the book. Going ahead, to turn in one direction, you need room on the other side for the stern to swing. This poor fellow [Diagram 4-5] needs to make a sharp turn to starboard, but has forgotten that his stern will swing to port as he does so. Going astern, it is the bow that swings out. The amount of room you need will vary with the conditions; do not count on it being the same from one occasion to the next.

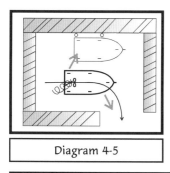

Diagram 4-5

Leave even *more* other-end room when the wind is gusty. The breeze is guaranteed to pick up just as you are about to execute your cleverly conceived turn; it will blow you sideways and use up your swinging room.

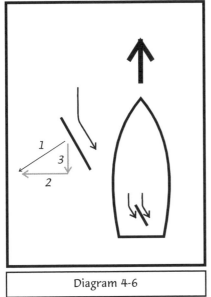

Diagram 4-6

Rudders

A sailboat steers by deflecting water to one side or the other with its large rudder [Diagram 4-6], creating this equal-and-opposite reaction business that is one of the Laws of Motion. The (optional) vector diagram shows the resultant force on the rudder (1), and breaks it down into a lateral (turning or yawing) force (2), and drag (3). (The more forceful the turn, the higher also the drag.) Putting the rudder to one side turns the boat to the same side. This is true whether making headway or sternway (although the boat's *ends* will swing differently — see above).

Moving the rudder to starboard or to port is called, respectively, 'starboard helm' or 'port helm'. A steering wheel is turned to the same side as the rudder, and a tiller, shown by the more lightly shaded line [Diagram 4-7], to the opposite.

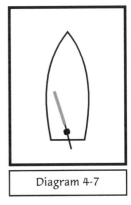

Diagram 4-7

You already know (although it has not occurred to everybody else!) that if the boat is not moving, relative to the water, it cannot be steered. Water has to flow by that rudder. At times, a sailboat may not have much water speed with which to steer. Hence, the rudder needs to be relatively large. Conversely, a power boat, built for higher speeds, has a smaller rudder for optimal performance — optimal at cruising speeds, that is. At docking speeds, and/or when coasting in neutral gear, the rudder may not provide all of the steering authority which one would wish.

Discharge Current

The situation changes considerably when engine power is added. The propeller, in forward gear, shoots a column of water, the 'discharge current', backwards with considerable force. The rudder is placed behind the propeller, in the discharge current, to amplify its steering effect [Diagram 4-8]. Much more water will flow by the rudder than would do so just due to the movement of the hull through the water. That is why power boats tend to have smaller rudders than sailboats, and why most twin screw vessels have *two* rudders, one behind each propeller, rather than one in the midline.

You can see that an underpowered boat, with too small an engine or propeller, will steer less well. 'Underpowered' is a relative term

Diagram 4-8

here; 'mismatched' might be better. If, for a given hull and rudder, the power available is insufficient, you may have less than decisive steering control.

Small sailboats often have a little outboard engine, for auxiliary power. They lose a little, by not having the rudder in the discharge current, and gain a little because the motive force itself can swivel.

Not only does the discharge current confer a stronger steering effect from a smaller rudder, but it also confers the ability to turn with no way on! (Having 'no way on' is nauticalspeak for 'not moving'). Even though a boat has neither headway nor sternway, the propeller is shooting a discharge current past the rudder; and one can still steer.

How can a boat not be moving, if the propeller is turning? There are several ways. It may be that you had been backing up, and now are using forward gear as a 'brake'. It may be that you have some lines on the pier, but are using power to maneuver yourself in closer or out farther (see the section on power spring lines), in preparation for tying up or departing.

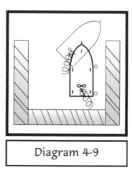

Diagram 4-9

Most importantly, the boat may be just *starting* to get under way [Diagram 4-9], under which circumstance you can often turn it quite sharply while making minimal headway. This can be very useful for turning with limited room. Although a brief, decisive 'vroom' from your engines can be disturbing to those docked nearby, it may be just the thing to get your boat realigned and out of harm's way, without picking up any appreciable speed.

It's incredible to see large sailboats do this under power. Many of them can turn almost on the spot, at slow speeds, even ones with long keels. One would not necessarily think them all that maneuverable just to look at them. It partly results from their big rudders, which give them strong steerage and, with large deflections, high drag.

This does not work as well in a faster boat, up at cruising speed. The hull will be 'tracking', and will resist such a tight turn, vigorous throttle and rudder work notwithstanding.

Just a Little Faster

'Steerageway' is the speed at which enough water is moving by the rudder that the boat can be steered. When conditions are unfavourable, you may need stronger steerage, and so may need to be moving faster. This can be unsettling to nearby boaters, and the many who disagree with this technique *do* have a point. But watch professionals, or the more successful and experienced dockers around you, and you will see many who are moving into dock quite quickly.

One reason they do this is so they can steer. Another reason is to provide momentum (linear and/or angular), with which to complete the approach and/or the turn to the dock. Momentum can be handy for overcoming adverse forces which might try to spoil your approach just as you come to a stop.

Going faster is a trade off. If you hit anything, you will hit harder. If your engine stalls, or you fumble the controls (you?!), you have gone from being in trouble to being in worse trouble. Also, you may need more reverse gear to stop, which can present its own steerage problems.

Therefore, this is not to suggest that you race into dock. No, by no means should you charge around a marina at high speed. The speeds I am speaking of are still slow, minimal wake speeds; they are just not as slow as idle speed. Any wake you produce will not only antagonize moored boaters, but can also wash up under your own boat as you slow to a stop, and move it around rather violently.

The speed at which you should perform close quarters maneuvers is the slowest at which you can maintain positive control of your vessel. In calm conditions, this likely will be idle speed. Much of your jockeying may, in fact, be in neutral gear, coasting along ever so slowly until another brief push is needed. At other times, you may need to go just a little faster than you think. Although it may on occasion seem reckless to pick up the pace, it can, in fact, be more reckless to lack adequate rudder authority.

Even proceeding at dead slow speed, you still can and may need to use short bursts of power to steer and to maintain alignment.

Cushions of Water

A water cushion can develop between the boat and any other *solid* object. A hull in motion moves water out of the way, and some of this water is pushed off to the sides. When one side is blocked by an immovable wharf, the water that is caught in between can push the boat away [Diagram 4-10], and impede its progress just as it tries to make that last little drift into the dock.

This effect is less noticeable at low speeds and with shallow-draught vessels. Also, many wharves and piers are open structures, through or under which water can flow, and then the water cushion effect will be minimal or absent.

Still, it is one of several factors that sometimes require the angle of approach to the dock to be sharper than one might think necessary.

Occasionally, this cushion is used on purpose, to help get clear of a dock. In reverse gear, before the boat is even moving, the discharge current from the propeller will move forwards and upwards, and part of it will come between the boat and the wharf, and try to separate them [Diagram 4-11].

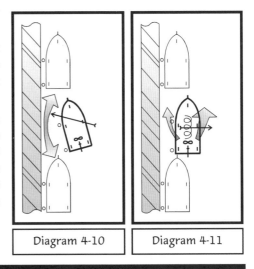

| Diagram 4-10 | Diagram 4-11 |

The scientific purists among you will notice that a moving body of water between the boat and the dock could, paradoxically, pull them together. This is the Venturi effect: the faster-flowing a fluid, the lower the pressure. (A boat scooting quickly alongside a solid, stationary object can, actually, get sucked into it. This is counter-intuitive for most of us, but that's the way it works.) In theory, then, the separation forces will be more likely to predominate with a big, low-pitch propeller, used for just a moment to get a large volume of slow-moving water in between the boat and the wharf. Try it with various throttle settings and for varying lengths of time (it usually will be only for a few seconds), and learn how it affects your boat.

Asymmetrical Thrust

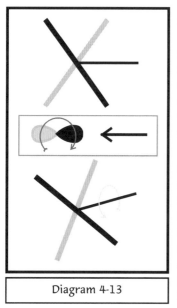

Diagram 4-13

The propeller itself often tries to turn the boat. Its thrust is *asymmetrical*, and the propeller is said to 'walk' sideways. Some authorities contend that its thrust is only asymmetrical if its shaft enters the water on a downward angle, although many boaters claim experience to the contrary. Outboard and sterndrive installations, for example, often have marked asymmetrical thrust which varies little with tilting the outdrive.

This asymmetrical effect is most noticeable at low speeds and with strong thrust — just the conditions one might encounter when accelerating, decelerating or pivoting the boat in close quarters. Various other sections of the book describe when it is that asymmetrical thrust is a liability, how to deal with it, and under what circumstances it becomes an asset.

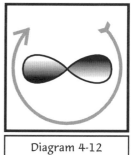

Diagram 4-12

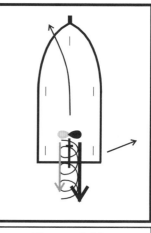

Diagram 4-14

Here is an admitted simplification of what turns out to be very complicated physics. Most propellers are of the 'right-hand' variety, meaning that in forward gear they turn clockwise, when viewed from astern [Diagram 4-12]. Looking at a right-hand propeller from the starboard side [Diagram 4-13], with the downgoing blade shown in black and the upgoing blade in grey, you can see how much the angle of the two blades begins to differ when the propeller shaft is angled downwards even only 15 degrees (lower

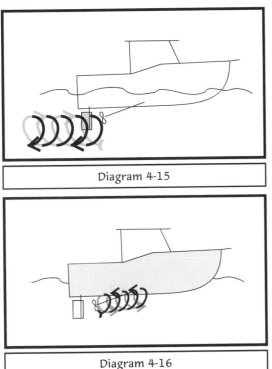

Diagram 4-15

Diagram 4-16

Diagram 4-17

schematic). The downgoing (starboard) blade, being more highly pitched, has more thrust than the upgoing (port) blade, and so throws the stern to starboard [Diagram 4-14], turning the boat to port.

Another important factor in asymmetrical thrust is that the discharge current is corkscrew-shaped [Diagram 4-15]. Quite often, the lower half of this corkscrewing cylinder of water does nothing more than churn water. (The *fore and- aft* propulsive force acts directly at the propeller blades — nothing else about the discharge current produces *propulsion*.) The upper half of the spiralling discharge current, however, usually impacts on the rudder and/or keel, and on the stern sections of the hull, and so causes the boat to turn. This effect probably largely accounts for asymmetrical thrust in the absence of propeller shaft angulation.

In reverse gear [Diagram 4-16], the asymmetrical discharge current affects much more surface area than in forward gear, and it's a surface area which is fixed, versus the rudder which is movable. The stern then goes strongly to port [Diagram 4-17], more so if the hull is of a deep-V shape or boasts a substantial keel. Some hulls and some propellers do this more than others, so if yours steers fine in reverse, just be joyful.

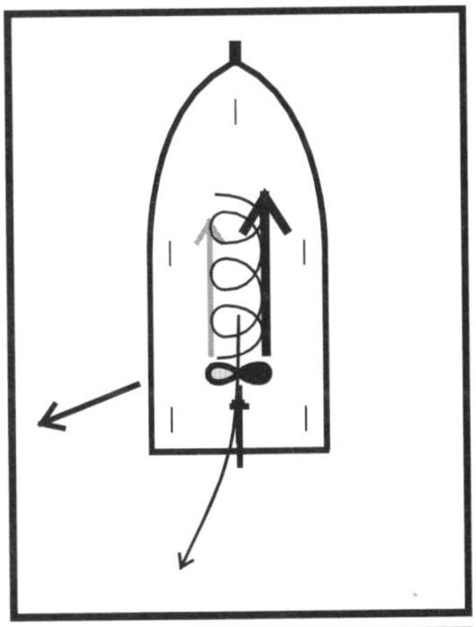

Outboards and sterndrives have no rudder, so some of their forward gear asymmetrical thrust is muted. Asymmetrical thrust is minimized also on some outdrives which have two counter-rotating co-axial propellers, i.e. both on one shaft.

Some boats, such as some inboard-engine sailboats, have their rudder shafts installed a little to one side, rather than right on the midline — this serves to make it easier to remove when needed for servicing (because the rudder is otherwise in the way), but the builder generally offsets the shaft to the side which will minimize asymmetrical propeller thrust, as well, i.e. to port for a right-hand propeller.

A sizeable minority are *left*-hand propellers, in which case you reverse the concept of asymmetrical thrust side for side.

Steerage Astern

Going astern is entirely different, under power. The rudder is now on the *suction* side of the propeller, and the suction current is broad and weak [Diagram 4-18]. The *discharge* current, now going forwards, is also less forceful, the propeller design often having been optimized strongly for forward, not rearward, propulsion. You know how much of a better 'bite' you get out of forward gear than reverse.

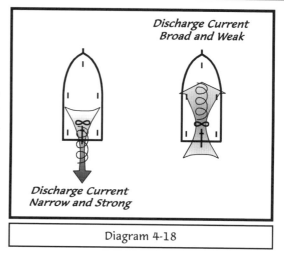

Discharge Current Broad and Weak

Discharge Current Narrow and Strong

Diagram 4-18

Here we are: the power boat has this smaller rudder, which now not only is not in the discharge current, but also has little water flowing by it, due to the boat's slow speed. Combine this with the potential adverse hull characteristics when steering astern, discussed elsewhere, and with asymmetrical propeller thrust, and you simply may not be able to steer well in reverse.

There are boats which cannot back to starboard at all, because of asymmetrical thrust, even with full rudder deflection, especially at low speed with vigorous throttle, such as when braking your forward motion, or when just getting sternway started. This can be discouraging, but at least if you know and understand how your boat behaves, you will not attempt things which it cannot do. Quite frequently, you can even use the side effects for your own purposes.

Once you get moving astern with some speed, enough water finally may flow by the rudder that some steerage can be effected, if the hull itself does not suffer from other astern steerage problems mentioned earlier.

On many boats, steerage astern is made more difficult if the trim tabs are lowered. There are several explanations for this, but once you think about it, you know intuitively that they will not help! (This doesn't refer to the sacrificial anodes on outdrives, also sometimes called 'trim tabs', but rather to the flat plates extending from the transom end of some planing hulls, adjustable electrohydraulically from the helm.) The drawing shows the port tab up [Diagram 4-19] and the starboard tab down, in both an oblique view and in a schematic side view. (The odd boater actually uses his trim tabs to *help* with astern steerage! — let's pretend we don't know him.) Suffice it to say that the trim tabs should always be left retracted (i.e. in the raised position, often called 'bow up') except when actually being used for boat trim while making headway. (Their mechanism also wears better if stored that way.)

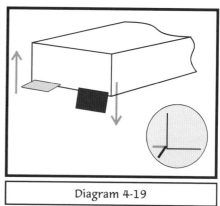

Diagram 4-19

Contrary Motion and Propulsion

What happens when the boat's direction of motion is contrary to the propeller's propulsion? It makes a difference whether you are i) making *headway* while in *reverse* gear, or ii) making *sternway* in *forward* gear. These two maneuvers are handled differently from each other. The (over-simplified) summary is this: In forward gear, steer as if you were making headway, whether you actually are or not; whereas, in reverse gear, steer by the direction the boat is travelling.

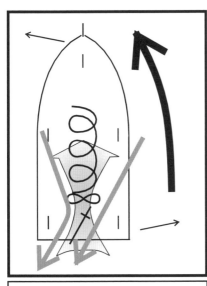

Firstly: Imagine that you are making headway, and then go into rever se gear, to 'brake' [Diagram 4-20]. For a short while, the boat will continue to make headway (large black arrow), and so at first the main effect on the rudder will be from the relative flow of water going by it from the boat's forward motion (two narrow grey arrows pointing astern). Remember that the propeller's suction current (large, broad grey arrow pointing ahead), which now is flowing past the rudder, is broad and weak, and its discharge current is going ahead, not flowing by the rudder at all. So, quite often, the rudder will continue to 'see' a current flowing by it from fore to aft, and you will continue to steer 'normally' (although the effect will be weaker than when in forward gear). Turning the

Diagram 4-20

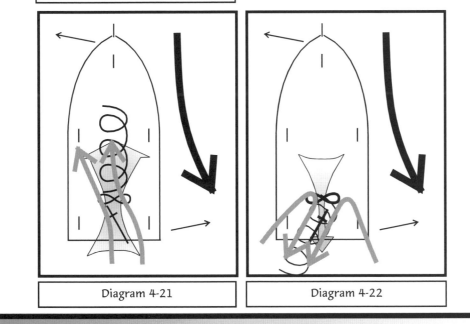

Diagram 4-21

Diagram 4-22

rudder to port still swings the bow to port, and the stern to starboard (small black arrows).

(Other forces will also be at work, such as asymmetrical thrust and the propeller's suction current acting on the rudder, and these may come to predominate as the boat slows down.)

Once you actually begin to make sternway, this all changes side for side [Diagram 4-21] (if you can steer at all!).

Remember the distinction between *turning* and *swinging* — in this example, the boat started out making headway, but in reverse gear. After it slows and begins to make sternway (still in reverse gear), you would turn the rudder from port to starboard, and the boat therefore would change from turning to port to turning to starboard. The boat's ends, however, would continue to swing as they were before — bow to port, stern to starboard.

Secondly: In *forward* gear, the rudder will almost always 'see' and respond to the propeller's discharge current, regardless of which way the boat is actually moving [Diagram 4-22]. So here you are, backing up, when, in the course of your maneuvering, it is time to go into forward gear. For a short while, you will still be making sternway, but your whole steerage changes, side for side, even before the direction of motion changes.

This is because the rudder immediately 'thinks' you are making headway — all it 'knows' is that water is rushing by it from ahead, even though the rest of the hull knows better!

So, while making sternway in reverse gear, you would turn to starboard to swing the stern to starboard. Still going astern, but now in *forward* gear, you turn to *port* to swing the stern to starboard.

Think about all of this for a while and you will figure it out. Doing it quickly and reflexively on the water is another matter! After the first thousand times it begins to feel more natural.

Steer in Forward Gear

*An important point to remember is this: although 'sternway steerage' is often difficult and unpredictable, you can steer in forward gear at any time, **whether the boat is moving ahead or astern**. When making sternway and having trouble steering, go into forward gear, straighten it out, then go back into reverse. You will often be able to realign your boat quite quickly, using the throttle and wheel gently but firmly, and usually without even beginning to make any headway — you will continue to move astern all the while. Do not wait to do this until the circumstances are critical; leave some room for the boat's ends to swing as you redirect your vessel.*

If it takes so much forward gear steering that you are making more headway than sternway, you may be attempting a maneuver beyond the capability of the boat or of yourself.

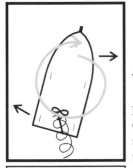

Diagram 4-23(a)

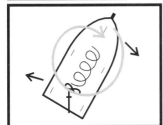

Diagram 4-23(b)

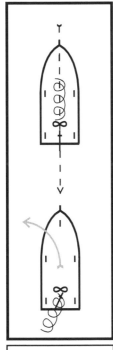

Diagram 4-24

Pivoting and Walking

Single screw pivoting

Many boats can come close to turning on the spot, although perhaps only in calm conditions for high-windage vessels. For a single engine inboard with a right-hand propeller, which likely throws the stern to port in reverse gear, you must pivot clockwise. Set the rudder to starboard, and leave it there. Give little shots of power, never enough to gain any appreciable 'way on', alternating between forward and reverse gears, and what should happen is this:

In forward gear, asymmetrical thrust notwithstanding, the propeller's discharge current, acting on the rudder, throws the stern to port [Diagram 4-23(a)]. (In fact, the rudder effect may be slightly stronger on this, the side of more powerful thrust.)

In reverse, ignore the rudder. It has negligible effect, now not in the discharge current, nor yet making any appreciable sternway through the water. This is fortunate, because otherwise you would have to move it to port to continue the pivot. The stern, however, moves to port because of the asymmetrical propeller thrust [Diagram 4-23(b)].

Go back into forward gear, and so forth. You are pivoting. Do a few 360's, and impress the crowd.

You can come close to pivoting by turning ahead after making sternway [Diagram 4-24]. Your backwards momentum combined with your forward turn will give a very sharp yaw, albeit perhaps only for 90 degrees, after which you will begin to make significant headway.

Twin screw pivoting

This alternating reverse–forward gear maneuvering is similar to that done by twin screw vessels. With two propellers on different shafts, however, you don't need to alternate: one side can be in forward gear and the other in reverse simultaneously.

At cruising speeds, one uses the twin screw effect infrequently; the more common application is for slow speed steerage.

Going ahead or astern on one propeller only, the boat yaws simply because of the off-centre position of the thrust [Diagram 4-25]. By going in forward gear on one engine and reverse on the other, turns can be done almost on the spot [Diagram 4-26]. The reversing engine may have to be run a bit faster than the forward one, because most propellers have a

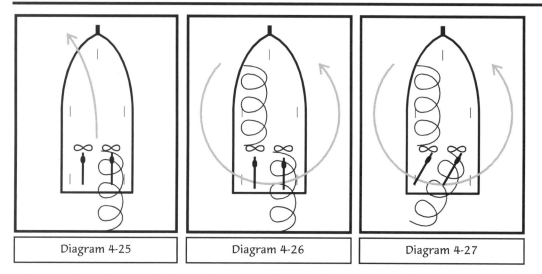

| Diagram 4-25 | Diagram 4-26 | Diagram 4-27 |

better grab on the water in forward gear. By adjusting the relative speeds of the two engines, the boat can also turn while making some headway or some sternway.

While twin screws do make close quarters maneuvering easier, often *much* easier; they do not absolve the helmsman from understanding the mechanics of docking. They actually can lead to trouble by engendering a false sense of security, and many a boater has strayed into danger by overestimating either their boat's or their own ability.

For example, it can require some very energetic throttle work to turn into a strong wind. Do not get caught in a forceful crosswind with no maneuvering room. With some boats, it may churn considerably less water to turn head to wind using forward gear only, on one or both engines, with the wheel hard over, albeit requiring more 'sea-room'.

You have to experiment with your own boat to decide what best to do with your rudders, as you steer by twin throttles. On some vessels, it is decidedly advantageous to use your rudder to augment the effect of the forward-gear engine [Diagram 4-27], because the discharge current helps the turn more than the rudder on the reversing side hinders. On others, for example with many twin inboard/outboards, the steering wheel is best left centered. If so, eliminating rudder control can be a disadvantage of maneuvering by throttle.

Twin inboards generally have better turning leverage than twin outboards or sterndrives. The diagrams are a bit complicated [Diagram 4-28], and so are included just for interest. The further forward the propellers, the higher the angle

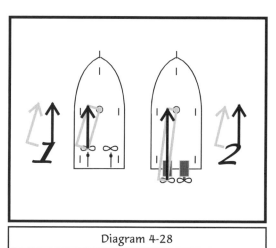

| Diagram 4-28 |

from them to the pivot point, and although this results in a shorter lever arm, the *rotational* component of thrust is higher with inboards (1) than with outboards (2). Inboard propeller shafts are often further apart laterally than their outboard/sterndrive cousins, which also confers a mechanical advantage upon them.

Anyway, the final result is that twin *inboards* will often give you better close quarters control than twin outboards. (Notice, though, how little of the thrust actually contributes to rotation, in either case.)

Inboard twin screws have long been mostly counter-rotating [Diagram 4-29]: the port propeller is a left-hand one, so that its inherent turning characteristics are the reverse of the standard right-hand one, discussed earlier. A left-hand propeller throws the stern to port in forward gear, and to starboard in reverse. The *intrinsic* and *positional* asymmetrical thrusts thus work together. Sterndrive twins, and some outboards, have increasingly been built this way for the last few years, but many such installations do not counterrotate. In this case, one depends solely on the off-centre position of the port screw to overpower its asymmetric thrust.

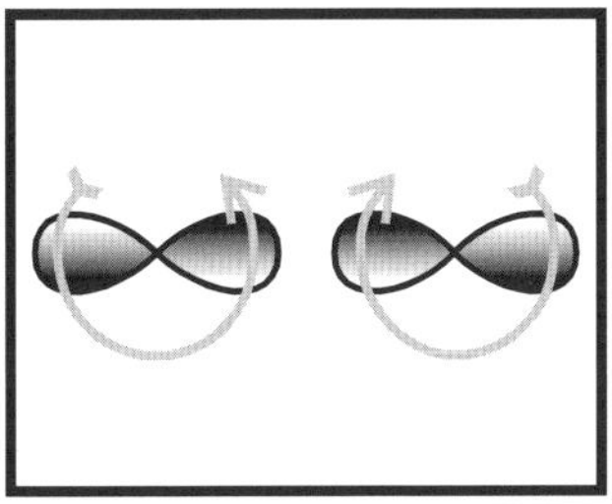

Diagram 4-29

Twin screw walking

Some twin screw boats, under some circumstances, can be made to go through the water sideways. (Could we say that they have 'sideway', as opposed to headway or sternway? Uh, no.) Whether they can or not depends on the balance of lateral forces to rotational forces; if you can make the sideways force a little stronger than the pivoting one, you can 'walk' your boat.

To move to port, for example, put the starboard engine into forward gear and the port into reverse [Diagram 4-30]. This will push the bow to port, but the walking forces of both propellers (the asymmetrical thrust) will move the stern to starboard. The vessel wants to pivot, and so you counteract this with rudder. Put the rudders to starboard, and the starboard propeller's discharge current, acting on the rudder in forward gear, might be able to overcome the walking forces of asymmetrical propeller thrust. If so, both ends of the boat are now being pushed to port.

You adjust the throttles and rudders as you go, maintaining alignment.

Many boaters claim to be able to position their vessels stern to in a slip this way, holding their position against a crosswind of fifteen knots or more. Some single-handers then leave the helm to attach one or two critical lines quickly, before returning to put the transmissions in neutral. You may question (as do I) the wisdom of leaving the helm of an unsecured boat with the propellers running — they simply say that they do what they have to do.

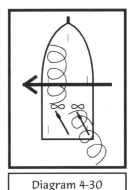

Diagram 4-30

So, you *pivot* by using the rudders to augment the propellers' asymmetrical thrust, and you *walk* by using the rudders to counteract it.

(The very best sideways walkers have their counter-rotating propellers reversed: left-hand to starboard, right-hand to port. The turning forces on the bow and the walking forces on the stern now work together. However, they do not pivot as well; only a few specialpurpose small craft are built this way anyway.)

Single screw walking

You simply cannot walk a single screw vessel the way you can a twin. It is much more difficult, and not even possible with many boats. You may, however, be able to use asymmetrical propeller thrust to help you shimmy sideways into a tight spot. Your crosswind tolerance will be less than with a twin screw, you will only be able to go to port (assuming a right-hand propeller). The larger your keel, the less practical this maneuver.

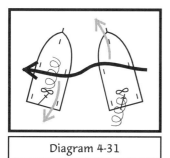

Diagram 4-31

Aligned with your slip [Diagram 4-31], go into forward gear with the rudder to port. This pushes the bow to port, but before you start moving ahead, shift to reverse. The propeller walks the stern back to port. The balance of lateral versus rotational forces is even more delicate than with twin screws, but if you and your boat have the ability, you just might walk.

Straight Line Stopping

Because of asymmetrical propeller thrust, your boat may yaw when you use reverse gear to slow to a stop. With a right-hand propeller it pivots clockwise. As you slow down you may have almost no rudder authority, and so not be able to control the swing.

Some boaters therefore turn to port before they engage reverse gear [Diagram 4-32], trying to correct in advance for the asymmetrical thrust. This is fine, although it's a little like 'walking', just discussed above: you will end up parallel to your original course, but set off to port.

So, if for whatever reason it is imperative to stop dead in your tracks, still completely aligned on your present course, you have to do a double shimmy [Diagram 4-33]. (It's fun.) Turn first a little to starboard, and then turn to port. Engage reverse gear, and walk your stern back on over to your original course, where you will stop.

Whew!

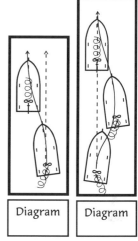

Diagram   Diagram

Outboards and Sterndrives

Outboards and sterndrives (inboard/outboards) differ somewhat from the inboard engine propeller and rudder configuration, although in many, if not most, respects the principles are very similar. And it makes you a better outboard engine boat operator to reflect upon the principles of inboard engine operation.

The big difference with outboards, of course, is that the entire motive force swivels, not just a rudder [Diagram 4-34]. (There is no rudder!) Therefore, in theory such a boat can turn more tightly than the same vessel with inboard propulsion.

Also, asymmetrical thrust is less of a practical problem. Nonetheless, some authorities contend that the asymmetrical thrust of the propeller will become reversed, side for side, when the propeller shaft is 'trimmed out' beyond the neutral position [Diagram 4-35] — now it is the upgoing blade which has the greater pitch (although the influence of the spiralling discharge current is unchanged and very likely will predominate). Compare the schematic in the upper right with the similar one in the section on 'asymmetrical thrust'.

Diagram 4-34

All of this is mitigated by the better backward steerage afforded by this rudderless arrangement. In reverse gear, whether going astern or still making headway, and whether the engine or outdrive is trimmed in or out, your propeller actually pulls the stern towards the side to which you want to steer.

Steering either ahead or astern with the engine(s) in neutral gear can be tenuous, however. The tiny skegs and the bulbous outdrive legs are no match for a proper rudder, so such a boat, while 'coasting', is often barely steerable.

Outboards usually have a tilt feature, sometimes lockable, for trailering or so that they can 'kick up' if they hit something underwater when making headway. However, in reverse gear, the tiltability can pull the 'leg' and propeller up to the water's surface (not useful!) if the throttle is opened too enthusiastically. Depending on circumstances, lock the tilt mechanism down or just use the throttle more gently.

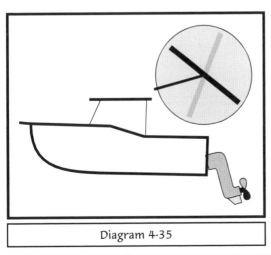

Diagram 4-35

Jet Boats

These things are reputed to be about as maneuverable as they come. The general principles of steering an outboard apply, although jet boats steer by redirecting a jet of water, so can often turn very tightly and quickly, and can also decelerate very briskly. They still 'skid' when they turn, and underestimating how much they can slide has often led to misadventure.

Some of them have unusual reverse gear steerage, and require turning the wheel in the opposite direction to that which you would with an outboard engine. For example, you may have to turn to starboard to back to port. It depends on the individual steering mechanism. There are variations of retractable 'clam-shells' [Diagram 4-36] which drop over the water outlet for reverse propulsion (upper right of diagram, showing water flow leaving discharger and reversing through clam-shell), and which steer much as a conventional rudder or outdrive does — in this case, turn to starboard to back to starboard. Some jetboats use swivels [Diagram 4-37], whereby the water discharger itself can be rotated more than 90 degrees to each side, to direct its flow forward. Notice that in the bottom left, the operator is turning to port while going ahead, and the boat responds, as expected, by turning ahead to port. Turning a little further to port, however, as in the upper right, initiates a turn astern to starboard. You get onto it after a while.

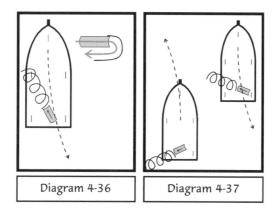

| Diagram 4-36 | Diagram 4-37 |

Chapter 5
— LINES & FENDERS —

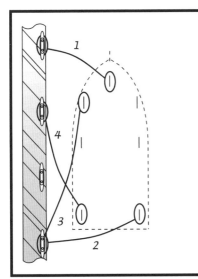

1	bow line
2	stern line
3	after bow spring
4	forward quarter spring

Diagram 5-1

Making Fast

'Making fast' is a salty way to refer to tying up a boat. We use **i)** bow and stern lines, **ii)** breast lines, and **iii)** spring lines [Diagram 5-1].

Bow and stern lines run out, often at a moderate angle, from their respective ends of the boat to the pier (or pile), and hold the boat in to the dock.

Breast lines (less applicable to small than large vessels, and so not shown) run directly *out* from the boat to the pier, and are shorter.

Spring lines run lengthwise *along* from the boat to the pier. They prevent excess fore and aft motion of the boat in its berth, or allow enough play in the line to allow for tidal ranges or wave action. In concert with the other lines, they prevent excess yaw, or squirming.

Spring lines have two-part names. The first part says which direction they run, forward or 'after'. The second part describes where they are attached to the boat: bow, amidships or quarter. So, a line running from the bow to a point further aft is called an 'after bow spring', and a line running from the stern to a point further forward is called a 'forward quarter spring'.

Remember that all mooring lines should go *under* the rail or life-line [Diagram 5-2], and then *outside* of all stanchions, shrouds, stays, etc. Otherwise, they are in the wrong orientation

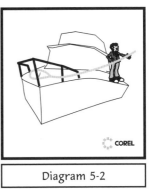

Diagram 5-2

when it suddenly comes time to use them. Even if you're standing on the bow when handling a bow line, it leaves the boat *under* the rail, and comes back *over* the rail to you.

Also then, bear in mind that you don't have to handle the line from its point of attachment to your boat. The placement of your cleats need not dictate the placement of your crew. A single-hander may hold onto a long bow line, for example, from anywhere on the boat right back to the cockpit, or the crew handling a larger vessel's stern line may stand at the ready amidships, neatly coiled line in hand.

A long bow line should not quite be able to reach the propeller, for obvious reasons! With amidships or stern lines, you often have no choice, but they are also the lines you are more likely to be able physically to reach, and so to keep under control.

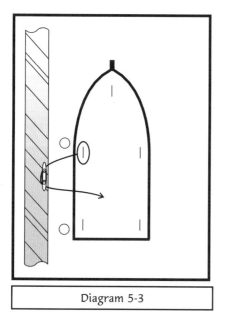

Diagram 5-3

Using a turn of a line around a dock cleat, with both ends secured or held on the boat [Diagram 5-3], allows the line to be cast off and pulled aboard quickly without having to leave the vessel, should the necessity arise (which from time to time it does).

It may be useful to have some preset lines for your usual home mooring. Tie bowlines or make eye splices, or whatever you want to do to feel seamanlike, at just the right lengths for some of your key mooring lines. It is often convenient to leave these lines at your home dock when you're away. They make it less work to secure and to unsecure your vessel, which makes the boating more fun, so that you will go out more often, and get better at docking! Make sure you have enough extra lines aboard to make fast properly when away from your home dock.

Keep more line on your boat than you think you will ever need, anyway. You always have the option of not using it, if you have too much, whereas the converse is definitely not true! A few *really* long lines can come in very handy, even if rarely used.

Unexpectedly, you may want very long spring lines, when big waves are unavoidable. You may need long lines if forced to raft up, two or three boats off a pier (see 'Rafting' below), or if you feel that some of your lines would be better doubled, or for anchoring or towing.

How long the lines?

Breast lines are not as useful for boats as they are for ships. I do not use them; even their temporary functions are better performed by spring lines, sometimes aided by power, sometimes by the wind or the current. In fact, one of my five hundred pet peeves is short mooring lines, and some expert boaters feel that there is never any justification for them under any circumstance. An exception could be made for an amidships breast line, left completely slack, and only used to pull the boat in closer for stepping aboard.

Your boat and its occupants will lie at dock more comfortably if its lines are long, with less stress on its structure as well as on the lines. I have seen very short lines part in two on more than one occasion, due to the repetitive and heavy snapping on them with every undulation of the boat.

You will see breast lines around, however, sometimes left attached, and sometimes just used temporarily while re-fuelling, etc., or while securing longer lines. Singlehanding in heavy weather, some boaters attach one breast line amidships, immediately on reaching the pier, just to hold the boat in the general vicinity. They may remove it as soon as other lines are secured. The reverse applies when getting under way.

Keeping your lines long is not optional in a tidal dockage. Long bow, stern and spring lines are the commonest way to keep the vessel in position, yet allow it to rise and fall, unattended, with any change in water level.

What Size Line?

Lines stretch, and the longer they are, the better shock absorbers they become. Smaller diameter lines are stretchier, other things being equal, so use lines big enough, but not too big. Here is only a rough guide:

Boat Length	Line Size
-to 22 ft.	3/8"
-to 30 ft.	1/2"
-to 40 ft.	5/8"
-over 40 ft.	3/4"

Type of line

There is no one *right* type of mooring line. The most expensive is not necessarily the best. For mooring, but not necessarily for other applications, I use nylon, twisted rather than braided, for the following reasons:

- inexpensive
- stronger than polyethylene or polypropylene
- sunlight resistant, unlike polyethylene or polypropylene
- stretchier than braided line
- stretchier than more expensive line (if shock-absorbency is important where you dock)
- handles well (double-braided is easier, though)
- *it came with my boat*

Other boaters clearly manage well with a variety of line materials.

How tight?

How tightly should you tie up your boat? This is as much of an art as a science, and it depends on the winds and waves that may be expected to blow up at 3:00 a.m., and on the stretchiness, length, size and number of the lines in use, on the tides, and on other things which {I cannot remember} are less important. Mooring lines and knots will often 'settle in' after a while, and more so after taking prolonged strains, so they may slacken after half an hour at dock, and then again after an overnight wind storm.

In general, keep your shorter lines, like bow and stern lines, a little on the loose side, and keep your longer lines, like spring lines, just barely taut. In a calm, non-tidal dockage, the vessel should be able to sit comfortably just off the dock in still air, and yet be able to move when the wind and waves whip up, without straining unduly at the lines nor crashing into the pier (liberal use of large fenders notwithstanding).

The length difference between a tight line and a slack one is sometimes very small, even as little as a hand's breadth! This, incidentally, makes it difficult to double your lines properly — if you use two lines together to provide more strength in heavy weather, then if one is even only a little tighter than the other, it may take most of the strain itself, and break, only to be followed by the (formerly) looser line, which now is alone.

If one end of your boat is near an obstruction, the vessel must be more firmly 'sprung' so as not to collide with it if (or when) conditions change while you are away from the boat. The stretch in the lines often will allow more fore and aft movement in rough weather than you can simulate, even with your admittedly impressive musculature, so leave some extra space at your hull's ends.

Similarly, if you have fenders adjusted to lie against piles, very little fore and aft movement can be permitted, and your spring lines will need to be more snug than otherwise.

Prototype Ties-Up

For most boats, a three-line mooring is minimal. There are many variations, but my favoured one [Diagram 5-4] is as follows: a stern line, led out from the cleat *far* from the pier (if your boat's cleats are suitably located) at about a 30–45 degree angle. This line at that angle also

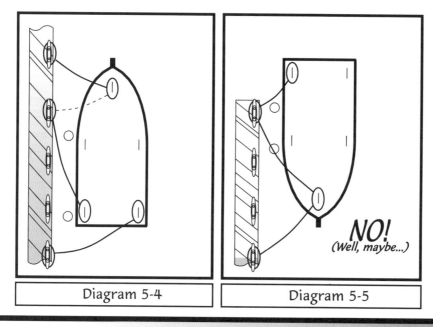

| Diagram 5-4 | Diagram 5-5 |

has some of the characteristics of an after quarter spring, in that it will resist forward movement of the boat. The next line is a forward quarter spring, which precludes movement astern. Make it long enough to be 'springy', perhaps two-thirds of your boat's length. And then, of course, the bow line holds the bow in.

The bow line would *usually* run forward (solid line), but *can* be attached abaft a little (dashed line), which can be handy if you are stern to in a dock which is shorter than your boat.

Attaching the spring line from a point further forward on the boat doesn't work quite as well. This might be called a forward *amidships* spring, and although it prevents movement abaft as well as a forward *quarter* spring line, it allows the boat to 'squirm' at moorings more than the line illustrated.

Reversing this 'short-dock' arrangement end for end is fine for some boats, but not so suitable for vessels with light bows and heavy sterns [Diagram 5-5]. The heavier stern will be more prone to flailing around, beyond the end of the pier, and it is harder to fasten the bow securely, because it curves away from the dock. It also restricts access to the dock from an aft cockpit, and allows the seas to bash into your transom rather than to part under your bow.

In rough conditions, or if your boat is larger, or if you will be leaving it unattended (or if you have a compulsive streak), then a four-line tie up is preferable (as in Diagram 5-1, earlier). This is my standard procedure. The added line is an after bow spring (or an after amidships spring). If your two spring lines are long enough, gently snug them up, and your boat can take some waves without undue strain. The stern line, then, relieved of the 'spring' component of its task, need not be at such an angle, and can go more directly to the dock. The bow and stern lines can also be a bit looser.

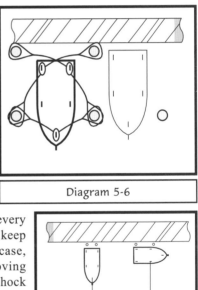

Diagram 5-6

The same principles can be applied to tying up to piles [Diagram 5-6]. In this example (remembering that every piling arrangement is different), the bow and stern lines keep the boat from moving much ahead, so one (or, in this case, two) forward quarter spring line(s) keep it from moving astern. (Notice also the crossed stern lines, giving better shock absorbency because of their length.)

'Cheater' lines to aid in docking between piles are described in the 'Pilings' section of the 'Docking Examples' chapter. They help in an adverse wind, or can be used manually to pull your boat into its slip. Now, these lines may not be in the best nautical tradition. The technique works well, however, and needs fewer crew, and no crew training.

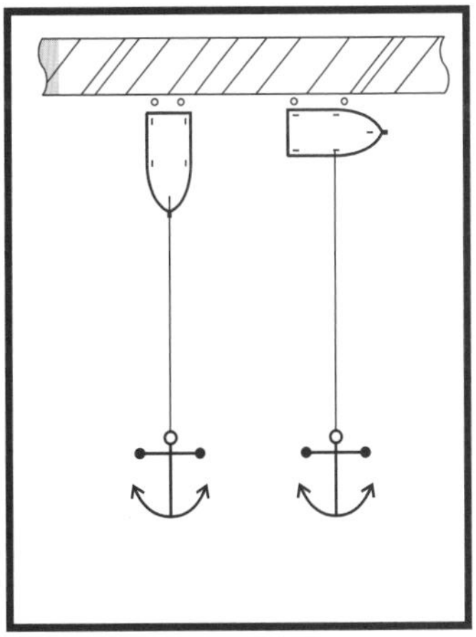

Diagram 5-7

Chapter 5 - Lines & Fenders

Shore-line and anchor combinations can be most useful, and their many applications are well worth investigating. An anchor can hold you off a pier in a pounding sea [Diagram 5-7], or allow you to make fast stern to ('Mediterranean mooring') when dock space is at a premium. Anchoring properly is an art in its own right, well deserving a book of its own (of which there are probably several in your local library), so make sure that you know how to do it before you go using it to assist you at your dock.

Knots and Loops

Learn some knots. Buy a book. Take a course. The ideal knot has several characteristics: it is easy to tie, does not slip, and, so that it is easy to *un*tie, does not jam.

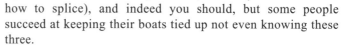

Diagram 5-8

The second knot most of us learned, after tying bows in our shoes, was the reef ('square', 'parcel' or 'flat') knot. Unfortunately, it is not as useful on the water as it is on land. You can get by fairly well, in terms of securing your vessel, with half-hitches, the bowline (this is a knot, not the same as a 'bow line'), and of course, the cleat hitches. Purists will insist you need to know twenty others (and that you should learn how to splice), and indeed you should, but some people succeed at keeping their boats tied up not even knowing these three.

All that we will discuss here are a few tricks that are often omitted from landlubberly knot instruction.

Bollards of the post-and-pin variety (shown here in top-down and side views [Diagram 5-8] with just a few turns of line on, for illustration) can be treated as if they were cleats on their sides.

You will sometimes want to tie a cleat in the *middle* of a line, if you wish to leave both ends secured where they are. Just tie a regular cleat hitch, as described, **except**, to avoid jamming, lock the *second* hitch, not the third, so that neither end of the line will pull directly on the locked part.

One end of a line is very often a loop or an eye. Depending on circumstances, you may want the loop ashore, to allow adjustment of the cleated end on your boat, or vice versa.

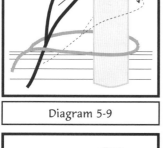

Diagram 5-9

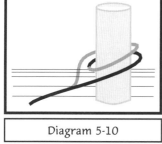

Diagram 5-10

The Cleat Hitch

The cleat hitch is often made much more complicated than necessary. The variation shown here, using a cleat and line in a top-down view, is much faster and easier to tie than other versions, very secure, and unties easily, even if left under strain for many months.

(i) Take one full turn about the base of the cleat, or at least have the line passing under both horns. Always start by going around the long way, not the short way.

(ii) Make one open (not locked) figure-of-eight (two crossed loops) around the horns, by starting with one half hitch, and then,

(iii) adding a second half-hitch.

(iv) Now, we're getting ready to add a final and locking half-hitch. (This is the only part of the knot that will have, or need, a lock in it.) Start by making a large, open bight of line clear around the horn of the cleat.

(v) Twist it into a loop **with the free end under**.

(vi) Snug the whole knot tight.

(vii) If you twist that last, locking half-hitch under the wrong way, you will see that it only crosses the cleat once. To make it cross twice, you now have to undo the twist a whole 360 degrees.

(viii) Conclude with another open turn around the base of the cleat, if only for tidiness.

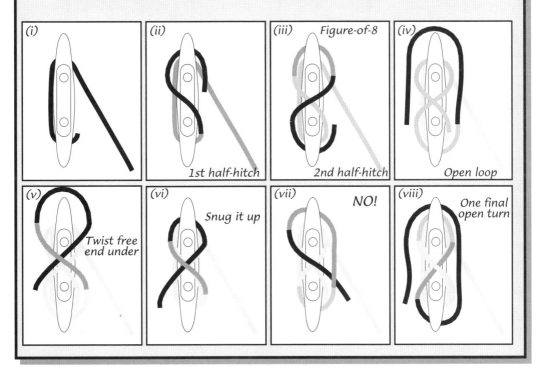

Chapter 5 - Lines & Fenders

If tying to a piling, most often the loop goes there. Note how you can 'dip' the line to avoid entangling it in others [Diagram 5-9]. Similarly, if you return to your docked boat only to find that the other guy, possessed of less finesse, has entrapped your line, you can 'un'-dip, pulling your loop up through his, over the post's top, then down through his again.

You may not want your loop sliding up or down the piling, perhaps to avoid chafe. Taking even only one extra turn with the loop [Diagram 5-10] makes it amazingly more secure. You can do the same thing with a loop around a cleat.

Rings

It isn't easy to find a good knot to secure to a ring. Half-hitches (minimum of three) go on fairly easily, but come out slowly, and can jam. Here's a simple one taught to me by an old salt, but not found in any reference I have encountered (so I can't vouch for it under all conditions, although my crotchet authority stands by it!)): pass a loop of line through the ring, and hold the loop over top of the standing part, as shown [Diagram 5-11]. Take one side of the loop (the side connected to the bitter end, the 'loose' end, not to the standing part itself) under the standing part, and then up through itself again.

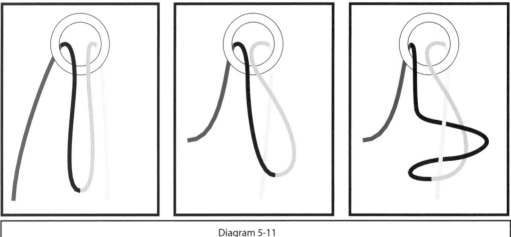

Diagram 5-11

This in itself is surprisingly good, although it has to slip for a while until it snugs itself up enough to hold. So, repeat the process at least once, or follow it with a half-hitch on the bight, which at least might not jam as firmly as a half-hitch right against the ring.

Tying with bights of line

A very simple, practical, speedy little trick is to tie some of your knots, or parts of your knots, with bights [Diagram 5-12], not ends. 'Bights' are just bends or loops in the middle of lines, and they can be handy especially if you are trying to secure a line which is much longer than necessary for the task at hand. Use the doubled end (to tie knots)

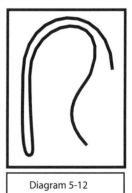
Diagram 5-12

as if it were single. They require lots of line (not just because it's doubled, but also because the knots end up so big), but they do not require you to be anywhere near the end of your line, nor to thread long lengths through rings or around piles.

Knots tied with bights are, as a generalization, also more secure than ordinary knots. They are particularly suitable for tying half-hitches.

Hauling In

The boat will have to be moved, at some point, by pulling on its lines. You may just be walking your boat that last little way into its slip. You may have decided that it is in as good a position as you can get it, so you are going to throw a line ashore and ask for a manual haul-in. There are a few ways to make this job easier.

Do not get tangled in the line (watch your feet especially), or **caught between** a tightening line and the boat or the water. Never put any part of a person between the boat and the wharf; the forces in there are considerable, quite enough to squish a body badly.

It often helps to take a turn around a cleat, pile or facsimile [Diagram 5-13]. This does not have to be anything at all fancy, just a turn of the mooring line passed around one or two cleat horns. Apply some tension to the line and the friction will add greatly to your ability to hold the line against whatever opposing forces, yet it interferes little with further easing out or hauling in. The line can be completely cast off with great haste, should the need arise.

Keep your hands out of the cleat. Learn to handle a running line close to the cleat, letting it slip through your hands as you work it quickly around the horns. This allows you good control without jamming your fingers.

Your leverage can be increased by a perpendicular pull on the line on the *boat* side of the cleat [Diagram 5-14]. This confers a mechanical advantage:

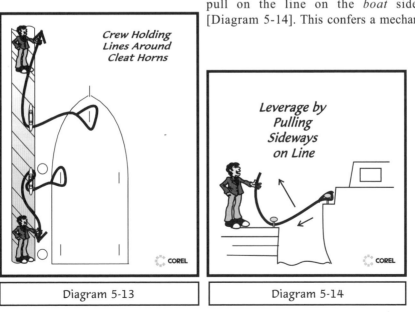

Crew Holding Lines Around Cleat Horns

Leverage by Pulling Sideways on Line

Diagram 5-13   Diagram 5-14

Chapter 5 - Lines & Fenders

you might reach down and pull on the line for a distance of three feet (at the long arrow), but the boat only moves one foot (short arrow). You have made yourself three times stronger. Next, relax your sideways pull, quickly and simultaneously hauling in the slack with your other arm. This can be done before the boat moves away again, and then holding the line around the cleat, as described above, maintains the gains you have made! (The same technique can be used to haul in an anchor line.)

Remember that when you pull on a bow or stern line, the rest of the boat will move too. Be prepared to protect the boat at the corner of the dock, and to manage the swing of the boat's 'other' end.

Unless you really have a long way to haul your vessel, take it easy and go slowly. **Note:** even a visibly slack line often carries enough tension to move the boat, so if the water and wind are calm, just give a little, steady tug, and it will gradually gather speed. As it gets some 'way on', pull even more gently — the boat will continue moving. You will often see some poor scurvy knaves straining away, their lines taut, as they haul a boat along a quay. It was slow to get it in motion, and then it does not occur to them, as it picks up more and more speed, that they will not be able to get it stopped when they want to! Dramatic, yes — seamanlike, no.

The Power of Power

*Try this experiment: with all of your usual dock lines **attached**, put your boat into gear at idle speed **only**. Then, from the dock, try to pull it by hand **against** its propulsion. You will be surprised at the force your engine and propeller are exerting — a larger cruiser may overpower you completely.*

***HEY!** Make **very** sure that your lines are securely attached, and will stay so, before putting the transmission in gear, and especially before stepping off the vessel — better to leave someone at the helm, for safety.*

The power haul

Your recreational ocean liner has to be walked back half a boat length, for instance. Despite being in heavy weather, the ends of the boat are under control, with the crew, on land, holding bow and stern lines. They start hauling the boat back, against the wind, their tired muscles aching and their soaking feet slipping on the wet pier, while you just sit there at the helm, perhaps mustering the energy to give gestures and words of encouragement.

Why not help them? It may not be possible to back up under power alone, without the wind blowing you away, but you can still go into reverse gear, and leave your crew to the easier task of maintaining alignment.

CAREFUL!! Very strong mechanical forces can be put into motion this way. Don't take the crew by surprise, or they could get badly hurt (caught in lines, squeezed between the boat and wharf, etc.). Be prepared to coast much or most of the way, to prevent picking up excess speed. Use forward gear to stop: if it was hard to get the vessel moving, it will be hard to stop it.

This principle applies equally to moving the boat ahead, and even to turning it — there are times when you wouldn't want to attempt a maneuver under power alone, but that doesn't mean you can't use power to assist your crew with their line work.

Power spring generalities

The techniques of powering your boat into position *with lines attached to the dock* are very useful, under-utilized docking tools. They seem to be just beyond the comfort level of many recreational boaters, and they usually (not always!) *do* require crew.

Used along with engine power, spring lines can help you to do some elegant maneuvers that otherwise can be quite difficult. You can avoid some very dramatic muscular effort, heaving in on lines and fending off from dock corners. You can hold your boat where you want it, once you get it there, without the wind or current undoing all of your fine helmsmanship before you can complete your tie-up.

A boat maneuvers poorly with just a *stern* line attached. Yes, the whole boat pivots, when turning, but the motive force is at the stern, and if you restrict it there, you impair steerage. A bow or amidships line is better. (You will remember that you can work with the free end of a bow line from the cockpit, rather than from the foredeck, if needs be. Keep it well secured: you definitely do not want it dragging overboard.)

When using engine power, the spring line and its attachments are subject to some very strong forces, easily able to overpower the human frame. This is often true even with the engine at idle speed, and the boat going dead slow. The lines and hardware must be in excellent working order, and even then can be damaged if due care is not taken.

WARNING!! Take all strains gently, and never get up any speed at all. You may have to let the engine into gear only for a moment, every few seconds, as the line tightens. This is especially important just as the line reaches its limit. Have the transmission in neutral at least for this instant, and then immediately put it back into gear at idle speed before the line slackens. Similarly, if using this technique to bring your boat into the dock, use neutral gear at least at the moment of impact, if not more often, to keep things slow, and forces mild.

Using spring lines with power requires caution and close attention. They are definitely only very temporary lines, to be left on long enough for you to attach something else. Always, always, check and double-check that the line is holding, that it is not slipping from any of its several attachments, and that the boat is staying where you expect it to. *Stay with the boat*; you surely do not want it wandering around the marina on its own, under power, having somehow self-undocked while you were away buying ice or whatever. Do not even get off the boat, to fiddle with your lines, for example, until you are absolutely positive that the arrangement is stable. If it fails, you must be prepared to start driving the boat without hesitation, and without tangling any dragging lines in your propeller. Bear in mind that if anyone falls overboard at the stern, there is a running propeller in the water there!

Also, power springing demands even more than usual attention to adequate fendering.

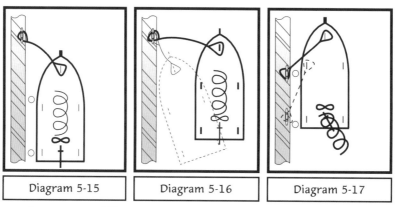

| Diagram 5-15 | Diagram 5-16 | Diagram 5-17 |

Power spring specifics

There are only a few basic power spring techniques which I would like to mention. Many other more advanced ones remain, and are worthy of study, but those presented here will suffice for most situations.

The first is **reversing on a forward bow spring** [Diagram 5-15]. This *holds* the boat in, parallel with the dock. It also is supposed to be able to bring the boat in, from a distance out, remaining parallel all the while [Diagram 5-16], but in practice, the pull on the line can bring the boat in rather heavily on the bow (dashed line), delicate operation of the vessel notwithstanding. Even when it does work well, it is difficult to attach if you are single-handing.

Secondly, a more versatile power spring line is the **after bow spring** [Diagram 5-17]. Turn the wheel away from the dock, and go ahead with the engine. Again, although the theory states that this line can bring you in, against a wind, for example, it also tends to pull many boats in bow-first, regardless of anything you can do with the helm. It helps somewhat to use a line from a cleat a little abaft of the bow (dashed line), if your boat has one. Either line, at least, certainly will hold you in against a pier, once you get there.

Thirdly, one **can reverse on a forward quarter spring** [Diagram 5-18] to back between piles, for example, or around the corner of a dock, in an unfavourable wind or with a recalcitrant vessel, or to pry your bow away from the dock prior to undocking (see the 'Docking Examples' chapter). You have more or less disabled the effect of the rudder by doing this, but it isn't needed for this maneuver anyway. The boat may have to nestle up to a pile, so adequate fendering is required. This line is often difficult to manage single-handedly — you sometimes need to be at the helm and handling the line simultaneously.

These power springs sound easy on paper, but they all require considerable practice, and fast, accurate work, to make them succeed, let alone to render them graceful.

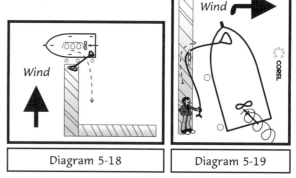

| Diagram 5-18 | Diagram 5-19 |

The 'Low-Line'

My own variation on the after bow spring, for single-handing, is the 'after double' spring line [Diagram 5-20]. It has a loop at both ends, one of which is attached to the stern cleat, and the other to either the bow or amidships cleat, depending on the boat. I then get a bight of line, somewhere nearer the stern end, and put it over a dock cleat. Going gently ahead, with only a bit of rudder (if any), springs some boats in more gently and more parallel to the dock than does an after bow spring.

If necessary, the loop at this line's stern end can be detached from the boat, and held out on a boat hook, to get it around the dock cleat. Then, it is pulled back in to the cockpit [Diagram 5-21] to be re-attached to the stern cleat. As you are hauling in, you are pulling both the bow and the stern in, and doing so with good mechanical advantage!

The after double spring line may be impractical to use with rings or with tall piles. This line chafes itself at the dock cleat, so, in addition to the previous warnings about power spring techniques, is clearly not suitable to be left on for more than a very short while.

*The Low-Line can be very useful without power, too. If you have enough time and can reach the dock, get off the boat, holding the line. **Do not get between the line and the boat** — take the line **after** you. You can, by holding on further ahead or abaft along the line, pull in on either end of the boat, and slide the whole vessel forward or astern. It's a versatile line!*

*When the boat is in about the right position, take a bight of line and secure it (to a cleat, a ring, a pile — whatever) [Diagram 5-22], somewhere in the middle of the Low-line. (See the section on ring knots.) Both boat ends are now under at least **moderate** control, and the vessel is well sprung against moving along the dock. Immediately perform a more formal tie-up.*

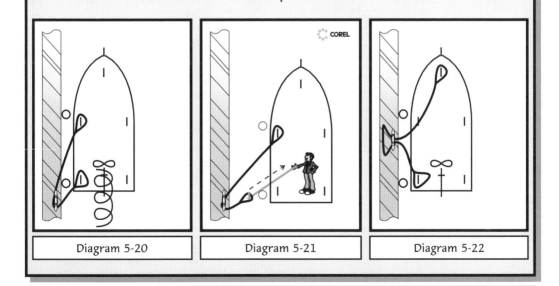

| Diagram 5-20 | Diagram 5-21 | Diagram 5-22 |

If you have a practised and experienced crew member on land, he or she can let an after bow spring *slip* a little, around a cleat, as you power the stern in [Diagram 5-19]. The boat will go ahead, so room has to be left for this, but the bow *might* not try to come crashing in to the pier as hard. The crew member will be surprised at the tremendous force applied to the line, and had better have it around two or more of the cleat's horns, to keep it from ripping completely out of his or her hands. Be gentle at the helm.

More commonly, the crew will simply fend off at the bow, but is often astonished at the exertion required to do this against the force of the engine, propeller and line.

Fenders

Fenders are cheaper than boats (or boat repairs!). Never approach a solid object, whether a dock or another boat or anything, without fenders in place. (Approaching *pilings* is a different matter — fenders can tangle in them while the vessel is still in motion, and their exact placement is not completely predictable in advance.)

Use good quality fenders, and if in any doubt about size go a little bigger. If in any doubt about number, use one more. *There are few side effects to too many too large fenders.*

If the dock extends higher than your gunwales, the fenders will usually be hung over the widest part of the topsides [Diagram 5-23]. If the dock is lower than the gunwale, have most of the fender below the dock level [Diagram 5-24]. This way, if the boat rises on a wave, the

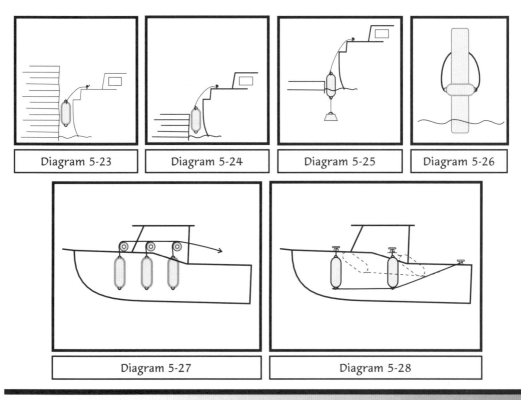

| Diagram 5-23 | Diagram 5-24 | Diagram 5-25 | Diagram 5-26 |

| Diagram 5-27 | Diagram 5-28 |

Whips

Whips are flexible poles (often made of fiberglass) designed to hold the boat off the dock in heavy seas. They provide an elegant solution for a sometimes difficult problem, although the vessel still needs to be well-secured with its regular mooring lines. Do not rely on your whips to do any more than hold your boat out at lines' length. Even then, boats have been badly damaged: make sure the whips are large enough and strong enough to deal not only with the vessel, but also the worst expected conditions.

If this is not possible, do something else. Choose a different location, tie up to a mooring buoy, or use an anchor to assist at holding the vessel off the dock.

fenders will not go high enough to flip up on top of the dock. The hull still remains protected in the *trough* of a wave because the fenders you have selected are big enough!

With very low docks, just above water level, you may float your fenders right over on their sides on the water's surface. This permits the hull to roll without losing protection. More elegant but more trouble (and rarely done) is to weight the fenders [Diagram 5-25], so that they partly submerge in the water. Take care not to foul your weights in the structure of the dock.

Sometimes, boaters attach fenders to the *dock* as well as to the boat. If the boat is secured against pilings you may want some of your fenders (whatever they're attached to) horizontal [Diagram 5-26]. Don't forget to retrieve them before you leave!

There are fender-attachment devices you can buy to adjust your fender height quickly, if you don't want to re-tie all of your knots. Some efficient boaters rig pulley systems, allowing adjustment from the cockpit of a whole set of fenders, with just one line [Diagram 5-27] (also not commonly seen). Whatever you do, attach your fender lines to something strong and secure, because when the boat rises on a wave while moving in against the dock, quite a bit of stress is applied to the deck fittings.

Once clear of a docking area, *take your fenders up*. There will be a lot of tongue-clucking if you don't, and at speed the fenders can slosh and bash around quite vigorously.

For those of us who single-hand in heavy weather, sometimes only going somewhere afew minutes away, walking all over the boat untying and stowing fenders is not practical. Inthis case, rig some sort of a retraction system, at least for the forward fenders that you cannotreach from the cockpit. The exact set-up will vary from boat to boat. You want something,usually, like a line connecting the lower ends of the fenders [Diagram 5-28], which runs back to the cockpit, and which can be secured quickly either tight (fenders up, dashed line) or loose (fenders down, solid line). Such a retraction system can be relatively unobtrusive, and because of its ease of operation, the fenders are more likely to be used.

Fender boards

Consider making and carrying a set of fender boards [Diagram 5-29]. These are wooden planks used to protect your fenders themselves from rough surfaces, such as the walls of locks, or to prevent tangling when putting two sets of fenders together (such as when 'rafting' two boats), or when tying up to a single pile.

The boards, which are often made of scrap lumber, frequently are hung from lines which pass through holes drilled width-wise. A fender and its line are shown in the diagram's upper left, and a line for the

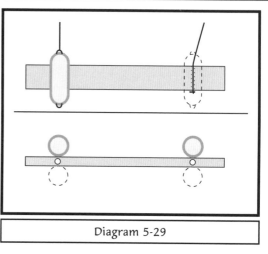

Diagram 5-29

board, which would be separate from the associated fender's line, is illustrated in the upper right. The fender board holes are shown end-on in the lower half of the diagram, with an optional second set of fenders (used if two boats are tied together and each wants to hang its own fenders) shown by dashed lines.

Rafting

There are a few little tricks to tying boats together, side by side. We often 'raft' for fun and friendship and sometimes just because there is no place else to go!

An anchored raft puts its largest boat(s) in the centre [Diagram 5-30]. As the raft grows, other boats near the ends may also anchor, and/or some might put

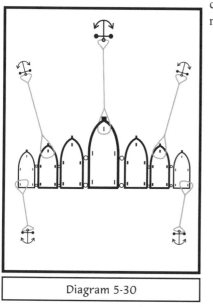

Diagram 5-30

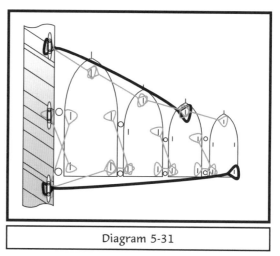

Diagram 5-31

out stern anchors. As each new boat joins the raft, tie it to the adjacent vessel exactly as if tying it to a dock — bow, stern and spring lines. When bow to wind, a particularly important line, to maintain transom alignment between boats, is the forward quarter spring from the outer boat to the *inner* boat.

Rafting is only for light airs and calm seas. Similarly, open water overnight rafting is ill-advised. It is better to hear than to experience the stories of being surprised by a late-night gale while rafted in open water. The larger the raft, the less quickly it can be disassembled. The more open the water and the more unpredictable the weather, the more you must be able to untether the raft quickly and have all boats promptly and safely underway.

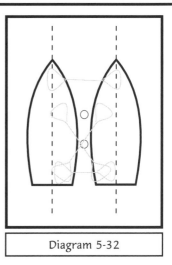

Diagram 5-32

Rafting at dock is similar, except that the largest boat goes against the dock. There are times when you can improve the stability of the raft by securing some of the outermost vessels directly to the pier (shown as more heavily shaded lines [Diagram 5-31]) as well as to each other.

The conventional wisdom is to align transoms. This keeps more of the line work and boat to boat transfers done from the cockpits, where it is easier and safer. It is also just tidier. Sailboats, however, have to keep their shrouds and spreaders out of each other's way as they roll in the waves, and so may intentionally misalign their transoms on these grounds.

Keep your centrelines parallel as well [Diagram 5-32]. This often means letting the sterns drift apart from each other a little.

(Remember rafting courtesy. You and the other boaters have chosen to be side by side, not on top of each other. Keep the noise down, and try to keep from scrambling over other boats any more than is needed.)

Coiling and Throwing

Learn how to coil and how to throw a line; these are invaluable assets for those times when people on land offer to help. A line is coiled most easily with a freehand technique [Diagram 5-33], not the around-the-elbow method. Start with the 'bitter end', the end that will be staying with you. For right-handers, hold it in your left hand, the line streaming away from you. You are coiling it clockwise (which happens to work out best for the usual three-stranded right-hand twisted line). Then, bring in a coil with your right hand, and lay it into your left. Again, lay it away from your body. This way, you are folding the line into a coil rather than twisting it in. If the line was already twisted, you may have to untwist it as you go.

The simple way to throw it is to hold the bitter end (the end you started with), in your left hand, and *do not let go*. (Letting go is embarrassing — if in a critical situation, consider tying the bitter end to the boat.) Move the rest of the coil to your right hand, and throw it with an under-handed swinging motion [Diagram 5-34]. The line will extend almost to its full length,

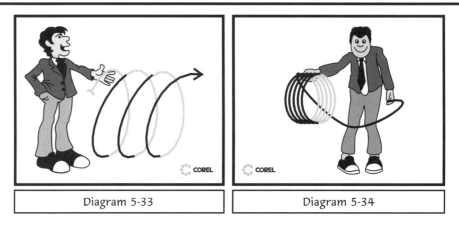

| Diagram 5-33 | Diagram 5-34 |

which it probably would not if just thrown as an uncoiled jumble. It is more likely to be caught successfully if it is long enough so that there is still a coil or two remaining when it reaches its intended recipient on the dock.

An even better way to throw is to hold only a third to a half of the coil in your right hand. Throw this, and let the remainder pay out smoothly from your left hand.

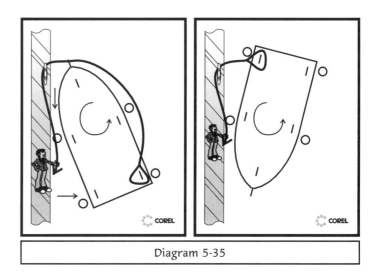

Diagram 5-35

Winding Ship

The exigencies of docking frequently require that we dock our boats the wrong way around, end for end, making it inconvenient or impossible to undock without turning the vessel around, or 'winding ship'. There are several ways to do this, some involving the use of engine power and some not, but here is a way that is very simple and can be done singlehandedly [Diagram 5-35].

Firstly, have fenders positioned on both sides of the boat. Take a lo-o-ong line, all the way around from the outer quarter cleat, past the bow, and then around a cleat (or ring or pile) on the dock. Now, start at the bow, and, depending on conditions, more or less work your way astern, detaching the mooring lines as you go. You are still holding onto, and keeping some tension on, your long line, and it will hold the bow in to the dock. Lastly, untie the boat's stern, and give it a shove out away from the dock. The only line still attached is the long one.

As the stern drifts away, walk back to the bow (keeping that long line taut), and grab hold of the boat, by the bow rail, for example. Slowly walk the bow of the boat along the dock, towards the spot where the stern used to be. At first, you may need to ease out a little of the long line, but very shortly you can start gently pulling it in. As the vessel comes around to an angle of about 135 degrees, you will slide your hold from the point of the bow to a spot further astern, allowing the bow's curvature to swing away from the dock. Pull the stern the rest of the way in, and tie or hold the long line while you get your other lines in place.

This procedure is slow — as long as you're making progress, it need not go quickly, so don't feel that you have to exert yourself strenuously. In fact, it's better not to get the boat moving too fast. At various stages, you will have to adjust the strength of your forces on the line and on the hull, and to adjust the direction of your force on the boat itself — at first, the hull needs to be fended off away from the dock, and at the end, the bow may tend to overrotate and need to be held in. A strong wind or current, if from the wrong direction, can cause trouble with this maneuver, but under most conditions it works well, and requires nothing more than advance organization (lines and fenders ready), and patience.

Chapter 6

— HUMAN FACTORS —

There are natural human instincts which often work against us in crisis situations. A difficult docking can provoke a most unpleasant emotional experience. The skipper, encumbered with the omnipresent fragile boater's ego, is only too aware of that valuable boat, and of those precious passengers. Panic easily ensues, and cogent thought becomes next to impossible.

Conversely, there is often so much to do and so much to think about, when a docking is not going smoothly, that the helmsperson may go paradoxically 'blank', intellectually as well as emotionally; he or she then ceases to think or to listen, just when either can be most necessary. Many boaters find it useful to learn to recognize and to acknowledge the signs of their own impending panic, and to work on some basic techniques to counter its effects.

If these references to high emotion when docking seem unfamiliar to you, the likeliest of several possible explanations is that you haven't done very much boating. My wish is for you to do lots of boating, and if you do, it is almost certain that eventually (and repeatedly) you and your crew will feel nervous, at the least, when attempting to dock the boat. The day this stops happening completely is the day you are no longer taking your boating seriously enough!

Now Calm Down

I don't know how to tell you not to panic. I do know that when you feel yourself flushing, your heart palpitating, your palms sweating and your knees wobbling, you are not going to be operating at maximal efficiency.

Remind yourself that your judgement will likely be poor. Make a conscious effort to calm down. Take a few slo-o-ow, deep breaths. Find that small, still inner spot of quiet and strength, usually somewhere near the pit of your stomach, depending on what you had for lunch.

A different approach is to harness that emotional energy to the task at hand. Try to trick your subconscious into feeling excited and vital, when it is trying to tell you that it is just terrified.

Pay Attention

So, let us say that you are able to relax. This doesn't mean that you should start discussing international economics just as you begin a difficult negotiation between your boat and its dock! Remain attentive, and keep your mind on what you are doing. Ask your passengers to let you concentrate on your docking.

It is usually obvious enough (to others) if you are not paying attention. More insidious is over-focusing. If you find yourself homing in on just one small aspect of a complicated docking, it is a sign that the stress of the situation is getting in the way of the bigger picture. For example, you get so caught up in getting yourself aligned for your approach to the dock, that you forget to avoid the rocks, or to continue your scan for other traffic around you, or to get your fenders out, or to talk to your crew, or to adjust the throttle or transmission. Keep the bigger picture in mind, and keep doing *all* of the things necessary to drive the boat.

Keep Thinking

Have a plan in mind, but continually reassess all of the many things going on around you. Be flexible! As you prepare to dock, new information may present itself to you, or the conditions may change. The boat may not be responding quite the way you had anticipated. You simply may come up with a better idea than the one you started with! You are not married to your plan; modify or discard it, if it seems appropriate to do so.

There is an old saying (which I made up): if whatever you are doing is not working, do something different. It is so self-evident that it bears frequent restating. If you attempt the same docking several times, learning more about the boat's responses to the present conditions each time, modifying and smoothing your technique, that's good. If you are all learned out, that's bad.

The 'something different' that you then have to consider could be any of a dozen or more things. The change could be large or subtle. You may not be sure what it is that has to change, but the weather and the laws of physics are more stubborn than you are, so unless something (*anything!*) changes, whatever did not work before will not work the next time.

Take Your Time

Now, you are relaxed but focused. You have a plan, but are not fixated on it. So, you will not feel in so much of a hurry. If the dockage or conditions are unfamiliar, circle around a few times, thinking it over.

Don't let a panicking crew rush you. (How to calm *them* down is another topic.) Go back out into open water, if need be, and discuss with them what you have in mind. Reset your lines and fenders, and give yourself a chance to collect your thoughts. Whatever you decide to try differently, give yourself enough time to discuss and to analyze what can be a very complicated situation. Unless the boat is sinking or is on fire, there is no shame in waiting, or in abandoning the docking and starting afresh.

Risk Assessment

This is one of the latest rages in business these days, and yet we find that the general populace still has some serious misconceptions about risk assessment. We're only human.

Nothing is without risk. What I am really advising here is simply to be a little more careful. Balance the risk of what you are doing against the possible consequences. If you are attempting a docking about which you are unsure, yet the worst outcome you envisage is hitting a bit hard with your fenders, you may accept it.

But, what if you estimate a small chance, say five percent, that you might crang your propeller on a rock? The risk may seem acceptable initially, but, looked on as damaging your screw on one in twenty approaches, it may not. A higher likelihood of a less serious event may be allowable, but even a small risk of a more grievous one is not.

Potentially disastrous outcomes should go hand in hand with back-up plans. The higher the risk, the more you need some idea of what you can do should worse be about to come to worst. If there are no 'outs', calculate this into your risk equation. There is no logic in performing a dangerous or uncertain maneuver simply because other boaters (or you) have gotten away with it before. Any sense of security that this gives you is *false*. They may have been lucky. **You may not.** They may have been among the nineteen out of twenty who, statistically, are going to get away with it, through no skill of their own. Or, they may actually be better at the helm than you (*them?!*), or may have more maneuverable boats.

Insisting on no risk at all will only serve to keep you shore-bound. However, we often see maneuvers performed more on hope than on any reasoned assessment of risk. Be very careful where there is any possibility of human injury or property damage. Do not hesitate to refuse to go in to some place of which you are not sure, whether others either have done it, or have assured you that you are able. Be comfortable within yourself that you are behaving safely.

Communicate

If crew work is part of your plan, the crew has to know what you are thinking, or at least what you want them to do. This sounds deceptively simple. In practice, with the wind howling, the waves crashing, and your thoughts racing, you might find it nigh unto impossible even to divert any mental energy for communication, let alone to make it effective.

There are many steps to good crew direction, but they merge quickly and seamlessly, on the boat. Some steps can be omitted or assumed if you and your crew are experienced, but not as many as you think! The steps include **i)** telling your crew what they need to know, being explicit, brief and unambiguous. So far, that is just about impossible, humans possessing the vagaries that they do, but let's just push on anyway.

Get their attention first, and then use terminology appropriate to their level of training. It can be hard to be heard, because sound only travels clearly over water when you don't want it to. So, **ii)** speak clearly, slowly and loudly. You have to **iii)** decide if they heard and understood your instructions, which often implies that you ask the crew to say them back again and re-explain them to you. Doing this without appearing condescending or snide qualifies you for sainthood, but the reality is that you cannot assume that you were heard or understood. Social graces or embarrassment frequently sabotage the clear exchange of ideas, often all the more so if the crew feels under stress.

Perhaps they did not quite comprehend what you said, but there is a crisis going on, such as trying to get into a tight, unfavourable dockage in a gale. So they may feel some panic themselves, and they do not want to bother you when you're clearly very busy and under stress yourself. They think (or *hope*) that you are in control of the situation anyway, and surely the other crew members know what is happening! You can see that just when the crew most needs to seek clarification is when it is most unlikely to do so.

You may very well need information and guidance *from* your crew, depending, for example, on such things as how well you can see over the sides and corners of the boat to the lines, cleats, piles, bollards, wharf, pier or bottom. The same principles of communication apply, although to some degree in reverse. If it requires several attempts to get your message and its reply understood, so be it. Very few people persist enough, when minds do not meet, but in a technically challenging and emotionally draining docking experience, if the minds remain mutually unacquainted, so may the boat with its dock. I will leave the social niceties to your own ingenuity; it is a matter of being assertive, not aggressive. It may very well require some polishing of your 'boat-side' manner.

Skipper's Perspective

An equally challenging topic is that of *taking* the crew's advice, once you have succeeded in procuring it. The crew members may be very experienced in their own right. They may have a different visual vantage than you, and they might, or might not, be better able to assess their own abilities, or lack thereof. However — *you* are still the skipper, ultimately responsible for the safety of the vessel and passengers; this gives you quite a different mental perspective from anybody else on the boat.

Quite often, your subordinates will display undue optimism, driven by the subconscious desire to succeed and to please. What if you want to know if there is enough water depth to get into a particular dock, for example? You may ask advice of someone on the bow, or on land. Be very wary of a reply like, "Well, I think so, I think you will be okay". That is only a very tentative 'maybe', at best. Even a more affirmative answer may mask a large degree of uncertainty. Even if you recognize this, you do not want to offend your crew, so in you go — crunch.

You may ask a crew member if he will be able to get onto the pier and quickly snub a line. He may have no idea, or even doubt whether he can, but he does not want to rain on your party, and figures you wouldn't ask him anyway if *you* didn't think he could, so he says yes. Splash. The crew is in the water. Crunch, again, the boat hits the dock, and then drifts away, unsecured.

Be polite, but more sceptical. Assume over-optimism from your crew, unless you have good reason to believe otherwise. One of your very valuable sources of information is your crew, but remember who is in charge, and *make up your own mind.*

Boat Docking

— CONCLUSION —

What you need now is to put lots of water under the bridge. Your progress will be faster as you spend time on your boat, operating it in diverse conditions. Examine others' handling and mishandling of their vessels. This book will make more and more sense to you as you refer back to it, comparing it with your own experiences on the water.

Landlubbers wonder why we even bother, if the whole topic of docking a boat is so involved. For boaters, the attraction of the water is visceral and defies logical explanation. It's like love.

And like love, a little skill and attention to close quarters maneuvering joyfully enhances the whole relationship. If you're going to do it, do it well. Learn the mechanics, and then practise them until they are a part of you.

Be careful. Take it at your own pace. Be easy on yourself, but always push for just a little better performance.

There are many facets to skilful, courteous boat operation. Learn how to dock your boat well, and many of your skills will carry over to other aspects of small craft handling. You will not only gain personal gratification and social accolades, but you will also increase safety to persons and property.

I hope that you have had an enjoyable voyage. Now, ready your lines and fenders, and prepare to bring her in to dock.

The END

Checklists

These checklists of mine have been developed over several years, and are products of both research and experience. They are simply tools that I have found useful for my own inland boating — feel free to adapt or to modify them to suit your particular circumstances, and to use them at your own risk as you best see fit.

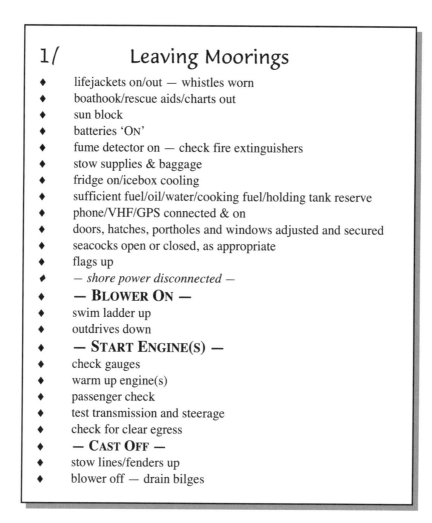

1/   Leaving Moorings

- ◆   lifejackets on/out — whistles worn
- ◆   boathook/rescue aids/charts out
- ◆   sun block
- ◆   batteries 'ON'
- ◆   fume detector on — check fire extinguishers
- ◆   stow supplies & baggage
- ◆   fridge on/icebox cooling
- ◆   sufficient fuel/oil/water/cooking fuel/holding tank reserve
- ◆   phone/VHF/GPS connected & on
- ◆   doors, hatches, portholes and windows adjusted and secured
- ◆   seacocks open or closed, as appropriate
- ◆   flags up
- ◆   *— shore power disconnected —*
- ◆   **— BLOWER ON —**
- ◆   swim ladder up
- ◆   outdrives down
- ◆   **— START ENGINE(S) —**
- ◆   check gauges
- ◆   warm up engine(s)
- ◆   passenger check
- ◆   test transmission and steerage
- ◆   check for clear egress
- ◆   **— CAST OFF —**
- ◆   stow lines/fenders up
- ◆   blower off — drain bilges

2/ Approaching Moorings

- ready fenders/lines/boathook
- test transmission and steerage
- have a plan and a back-up plan
- estimate course and ranges
- scan for traffic
- adjust mental state
- coordinate crew
- (outdrive raised)
- *pray*

3/ Tying up/Anchoring

- remove keys/adjust battery switches
- depth gauge/fume detector/other unnecessary electronics off
- adjust fridge
- adjust fenders

About the Author

Charles T. Low is a recreational boater in the Thousand Islands on the St. Lawrence River. He and his young family spend most of their summer vacations, weekends, and many evenings, on the water. Charles likes the beauty and tranquility of the islands, and also enjoys boating — an excellent match of process and product!

Other hobbies include photography, skiing, music, canoeing, camping, bicycling and computer programming. He is drawn to things that combine a technical mastery with an artistic sensibility.

This book was born of the frustration he encountered when first learning how to dock his boat. It started as informal research on the subject, with information culled from a number of sources. Now, it has grown into this more formal study of the skills required, and their underlying foundation, in terms accessible to every boater.

Much of the research was also simple observation of the successes and failures at boat docking which were going on all around him.

Charles is a full-time medical doctor, practising anesthesia, a rewarding and challenging career, except that it interferes too much with his boating (and writing)!